THE
FINANCIAL SECTOR
OF THE AMERICAN
ECONOMY

edited by
STUART BRUCHEY
University of Maine

A GARLAND SERIES

PREDICTING TURNING POINTS IN THE INTEREST RATE CYCLE

JAMES W. COONS

GARLAND PUBLISHING, INC.
NEW YORK & LONDON / 1994

Library of Congress Cataloging-in-Publication Data

Coons, James W., 1957–
     Predicting turning points in the interest rate cycle / James W. Coons.
         p.   cm. — (The Financial sector of the American economy)
     Includes bibliographical references and index.
     ISBN 0–8153–1777–8 (alk. paper)
     1. Interest rates.   2. Business cycles.   I. Title. II. Series.
     HB539.C774   1994
     332.8'2—dc20   93–49430
                                                              CIP

Printed on acid-free, 250-year-life paper
Manufactured in the United States of America

To Maggie

Contents

Preface

Someone once said that forecasting is very difficult, especially if it is about the future. Vast amounts of resources have been devoted over the years in attempts to overcome this difficulty. The state-of-the-art today relies on a heavy dose of statistical analysis, usually involving some form of regression application. The poor track record of forecasters, particularly when it comes to interest rate forecasting, is a serious indictment of such attempts. The purpose of the study presented in this book is to evaluate an alternative approach—the sequential filter—to managing the uncertainty inherent in the future course of the interest rate cycle.

The book has a direct bearing on the work of asset-liability managers in financial institutions, and is accessible to those with an undergraduate-level background in statistics. The application of the sequential filter to the interest rate cycle has relevance to portfolio managers, securities traders, finance professionals, and individual investors. All forecasters should have an interest in the general approach.

The study presented in this book was prepared and submitted in June 1990 as a thesis in partial fulfillment of the requirements for graduation from the Stonier Graduate School of Banking conducted by The American Bankers Association at The University of Delaware. The thesis was one of eight studies selected by a committee of eight senior-level bankers and academicians in the industry to receive the prestigious Library Award, based on the significance and originality of the topic, the clarity of presentation, and the thoroughness of the research. A revised version of the thesis was presented during the Contributed Papers session at the thirty-second annual meeting of the National Association of Business Economists in Washington, D.C. Since the initial study was completed, the methods described and employed have been used to augment the interest rate forecasting process at The Huntington National Bank in Columbus, Ohio.

The material presented in this book draws on the research of many individuals, but especially that of Salih Neftci. Neftci's clever application of A.N. Shiryayev's formula to the problem of detecting turning points in the business cycle offers an entirely new approach to forecasting. I am indebted to senior management of The Huntington National Bank, especially Frank Wobst, Zuheir Sofia, Don Stuhldreher, and Judith Fisher, for their support, without which this book would not exist. Ed O'Hara provided valuable suggestions for the outline of the research project and the writing of the thesis. My friend and colleague Al Pankratz made many insightful comments that kept the project on track. I was also fortunate to receive the thoughtful and patient editorial assistance of Robert MacKenzie and Chuck Bartelt. Most of all, I am grateful to my wife, who gave me immeasurable support and encouragement.

James W. Coons
Columbus, Ohio

Illustrations

Tables

List of abbreviations

ASA	American Statistical Association
CIBCR	Center for International Business Cycle Research
CIRCI	Composite Interest Rate Cycle Index
GNP	Gross National Product
LII	Leading Inflation Index
MAE	Mean Absolute Error
NAPM	National Association of Purchasing Managers
NBER	National Bureau of Economic Research
RMSE	Root Mean Squared Error
RPI	Retail Price Index

Predicting Turning Points in the Interest Rate Cycle

I
Introduction

To survive and grow, a major bank must make bets on interest rates.[1]

There is an old story that, in his travels, Albert Einstein came across three men with widely different IQs. The first had an IQ of 300. Einstein said, "That's great, Let's talk about my new theory of relativity." After awhile, he moved on and came across a fellow with an IQ of 150. Einstein said, "That's good, we can talk about global politics and the prospects for world peace." The third fellow he encountered had an IQ of 65. Upon discovering that, Einstein paused and then asked, "So, where do you think interest rates will be a year from now?"[2]

While interest rate forecasting has proven so difficult that it may be best left to simple minds, it is nonetheless an unavoidable evil for investors of all types: bond traders, portfolio managers, retirees, and young couples. Fluctuations in interest rates are of especially great concern to asset-liability managers at banks and thrifts, where the bottom line depends critically on maintaining a healthy spread between interest income and interest expense.

Interest rate exposure (the uncertainty of earnings due to potential changes in interest rates) can be eliminated by perfectly matching the duration of assets and liabilities. But, that is a complicated task in even a small bank, and unnecessarily limits the earnings potential of any institution.

As intermediators of credit, banks naturally encounter exposure to changes in interest rates. Indeed, one function of the asset-liability manager is to profitably control, not avoid, interest rate risk. The process of doing so, however, requires an outlook for interest rates.[3]

The attitudes of asset-liability managers toward interest rate forecasting span a broad spectrum. Some view a carefully formed interest rate outlook as integral to success, and undertake extensive research on the subject. At the other extreme are those who flatly refuse to speculate about the future course of rates.[4] Research suggests that forecasts can help in controlling interest rate exposure.[5] In addition, the use of synthetic financial products transmits the impact of interest rate fluctuations to credit risk,[6] heightening the importance of interest rate forecasting.

Unfortunately, interest rates are notoriously difficult to predict. The asset-liability manager typically faces the conflicting signals of intermittently reliable indicators and receives undependable projections from inconsistent sources. In part, the problem stems from pursuing a poorly chosen objective with inappropriate tools. Interest rate forecasts routinely specify single point estimates to an unrealistic degree of precision, even though predictions are inherently probabilistic statements.[7]

The most commonly used forecasting tools, such as ordinary least squares regression, are designed to predict conditional means, not the timing of turning points. The result is that conventional forecasting methods extrapolate trends into the future, without explicitly addressing changes in direction. In at least the case of interest rates, fundamental shifts are of paramount concern. "What a bank really wants to know is whether rates are likely to rise or fall; getting the forecast right down to the last 10 basis points is unnecessary."[8]

Moreover, while it is often important to consider the spreads between yields on different instruments, ". . . making the correct interest rate decision . . . can result in much larger incremental returns than a correct sector decision or astute issue or quality selection."[9] The fact that all interest rates move together over the cycle reduces the value of point forecasts for a large number of individual rates. The resources required to produce such comprehensive forecasts could be more effectively employed studying the likely direction for interest rates in general.

PURPOSE AND SCOPE

This book examines the ability of a technique from the field of sequential analysis to anticipate turning points in the interest rate cycle.[10] The approach, herein referred to as the sequential filter, has been used to generate signals of impending turns in the business cycle with some success.[11] The specific hypothesis is that the sequential filter can produce valuable signals of cyclical peaks and troughs in interest rates. The analysis is confined to U.S. interest rates during the period April 1953 to December 1988.

RESEARCH METHODS

A composite index of interest rates is constructed with the method used at the U.S. Department of Commerce to calculate composite indexes of economic activity. The index, named the composite interest rate cycle index (CIRCI), is a proxy for the interest rate cycle. The CIRCI is computed from yields on six instruments of differing maturity and credit quality.

Based on the CIRCI and a rule for identifying turning points, each month of the sample is classified as belonging to a period of rising rates (an upturn regime) or a period of falling rates (a downturn regime). The dates of peaks and troughs, which correspond to shifts between regimes, are used in generating benchmark forecasts, applying the sequential filter, and scoring the results.

The sequential filter is used to calculate the probability of a regime switch in each month of the sample period, based on values of an indicator series. A stopping time rule is used to extract optimal turning point signals from the probabilities. The usefulness of the signals is evaluated in absolute terms and by comparison with benchmark forecasts. The principal yardstick of performance is the portion of the change in yields during half cycles that occurs after turning point signals.

The leading inflation index (LII) is used as the indicator series. Economic theory holds that inflation expectations play a dominant role in determining the level of interest rates. In turn, the formation of inflation expectations depends on rates of inflation observed in the past. By serving as a proxy for future inflation expectations, advance information on actual inflation assists in anticipating turning points in the interest rate cycle.

The LII is compiled and published by the Center for International Business Cycle Research (CIBCR) at the Columbia University Graduate School of Business. The seven component series of the index are tied theoretically and empirically to fluctuations in the rate of inflation. In fact, the LII has a record of changing direction in advance of peaks and troughs in interest rates, as well as inflation.[12]

DELIMITATIONS

The focus of this book is the anticipation of turning points, not the prediction of explicit levels. The book also does not address the duration of regimes—the length of time between two turning points. In both cases, however, historical experience offers some guidance.

Second, the boundaries of the book exclude an explicit test of the sequential filter as a tool for asset-liability management. The inquiry is limited to the ability of the sequential filter to produce valuable signals of turning points in the interest rate cycle. Nevertheless, the findings imply that the approach would have provided guidance to asset-liability managers during the sample period.

Third, the book does not address the yield on a specific instrument. Instead, the CIRCI serves as a proxy for the co-movement among rates over the cycle. These synchronized fluctuations are assumed to reflect an unobservable element common to all rates, which in the abstract can be thought of as the "state of interest rates."[13]

LIMITATIONS

Monthly percent changes in the LII are transformed with the sequential filter into probabilities of a near term regime change. A regime change is the switch from a period of rising to falling rates or from a period of falling to rising rates. The exact timing of the change is not derived as part of the analysis, presenting some difficulty in its real-time application. For example, the occurrence of a peak signal indicates that a peak is imminent, but does not specify a precise time. In practice, however, lead times at both peaks and troughs have been relatively short and have varied little.

In addition, the book is *ex post* in the sense that it is conducted with some information that was not available during the sample period. The CIBCR revises values of the LII periodically, as the component series undergo benchmark adjustments by the original sources. Presumably, the revision process adds information that is not contained in the series when the data are initially released. Scholars disagree about the validity of conclusions that are based on revised data for real-time applications.[14] Since *ex post* analysis is common practice in empirical economic research, however, the use of revised data is considered a minor shortcoming.

Finally, the sequential filter is designed to signal only major turning points. Relatively large, but non-cyclical moves in interest rates might go undetected. The sequential filter serves as a means of more efficiently, thoroughly, and specifically interpreting the information contained in an indicator series, not as a crystal ball.

STRUCTURE OF THE BOOK

The book is organized as follows. Chapter II examines the current state of interest rate forecasting. The interest rate prediction problem is restated to reflect a more appropriate and achievable goal. The interest rate cycle is defined, the CIRCI is constructed, and the cyclical peaks and troughs are identified in Chapter III. Chapter IV evaluates four techniques for producing benchmark forecasts of interest rate cycle turning points, against which the performance of the sequential filter can be judged.

Chapter V discusses factors that affect interest rates. Inflation expectations are shown to have a dominant influence on rates. The attributes of leading indicators are discussed and the leading inflation index is described. Chapter VI tests the accuracy of sequential filter turning point signals during the sample period. Chapter VII concludes that the sequential filter of the LII would have produced valuable signals of turning points in the interest rate cycle during most of the post-war period.

NOTES

1. Marcia L. Stigum and Rene O. Branch, *Managing Bank Assets and Liabilities* (Homewood, Illinois: Dow Jones-Irwin, 1983), p. 259.

2. Adapted from Ben Weberman, "Smart Answers to Dumb Questions," *Forbes*, 19 May 1986, 110.

3. Stigum and Branch, *Managing Bank Assets*, 263.

4. See for example the description of Eugene Rotberg's interest rate forecasting operation at the World Bank in Ben Weberman, op. cit., 111 and "Gap Management Eases Interest Rate Swings," *Savings Institutions* 109 (November 1988): 46.

5. Michael T. Belongia and Gary J. Santoni, "Interest Rate Risk, Market Value, and Hedging Financial Portfolios," *Journal of Financial Research*, (Spring 1987): 48.

6. Katerina Simons, "Measuring Credit Risk in Interest Rate Swaps," Federal Reserve Bank of Boston *New England Economic Review*, (November/December 1989): 31.

7. Victor Zarnowitz and Louis A. Lambros, "Consensus and Uncertainty in Economic Prediction," *Journal of Political Economy* 95 (June 1987): 591.

8. Stigum and Branch, *Managing Bank Assets*, 227.

9. Paul H. Wilson, "Can Interest Rates Really Be Predicted?" *Pension World* 23 (May 1987): 18.

10. The rule is derived from a branch of statistics called sequential analysis. For an introductory discussion of the subject, see G. Barrie Wetherill and Kevin D. Glazebrook, *Sequential Methods in Statistics* 3d ed. (London: Chapman and Hall, 1986), A. N. Shiryayev, *Optimal Stopping Rules* (New York: Springer-Verlag, 1978), and Richard M. Cyert and Morris H. DeGroot, *Bayesian Analysis and Uncertainty in Economic Theory* (Towtowa, New Jersey: Rowman and Littlefield, 1987).

11. See Salih N. Neftci, "Optimal Prediction of Cyclical Downturns," *Journal of Economic Dynamics and Control* 4 (March 1982): 225, Carl J. Palash and Lawrence J. Radecki, "Using Monetary and Financial Variables to Predict Cyclical Downturns," Federal Reserve Bank of New York *Quarterly Review* 10 (summer 1985): 36, Francis X. Diebold and Glenn D. Rudebusch, "Scoring the Leading

Indicators," *Journal of Business* 62 (June 1989): 369, Francis X. Diebold and Glenn D. Rudebusch, "Ex Ante Turning Point Forecasting with the Composite Leading Index", Federal Reserve Board, Finance and Economics Discussion Series, no. 40, (October 1988), and Leonard Mills, "Can Stock Prices Reliably Predict Recessions?" Federal Reserve Bank of Philadelphia *Business Review*, (September/October 1988): 3.

12. See Geoffrey H. Moore, "An Improved Leading Index of Inflation," Center for International Business Cycle Research, Columbia University, Graduate School of Business, manuscript, (October 1988) for a thorough description of the leading inflation index. The index is published each month by the Center for International Business Cycle Research in The Leading Indicators Press Release. John P. Cullity, "Signals of Movements in Inflation and Interest Rates," *Financial Analyst's Journal* 43 (September/October 1987): 47 establishes the value of the leading inflation index as a predictor of inflation and interest rates.

13. See G. J. Santoni and Courtenay C. Stone, "Navigating The Interest Rate Morass: Some Basic Principles," Federal Reserve Bank of St. Louis *Review* 63 (March 1981): 11 and Sidney Homer, *A History of Interest Rates*, 2d ed. (New Brunswick, New Jersey: Rutgers University Press, 1977): 388 for a discussion of the co-movement among interest rates. The concept of an unobserved element that is common to all interest rates and is responsible for the interest rate cycle is equivalent to the notion of an unobserved variable that generates the business cycle, discussed in James H. Stock and Mark W. Watson, "A Probability Model of the Coincident Economic Indicators," National Bureau of Economic Research, working paper no. 2772, (November 1988): 1.

14. Diebold and Rudebusch, "Ex Ante," 15 and Victor Zarnowitz and Geoffrey H. Moore, "Sequential Signals of Recession and Recovery," *Journal of Business* 55 (January 1982): 77 disagree on the impact of using revised versus preliminary values of the leading economic index to predict peaks and troughs in the business cycle. Terry J. Fitzgerald and Preston J. Miller, "A Simple Way to Estimate Current-Quarter GNP," Federal Reserve Bank of Minneapolis *Quarterly Review* 13 (fall 1989): 27 discuss the impact of using preliminary or revised data in predicting quarterly GNP.

II
The Folly of Forecasting

When economists are asked for forecasts, they reply because they're asked, not because they know.[1]

History is replete with examples of economic forecasts gone awry. In testimony before Congress in February 1974, Federal Reserve Chairman Arthur Burns confidently predicted smooth sailing for the U.S. economy for the foreseeable future.[2] As it turned out, not only was his outlook optimistic, the economy was already nearly three months into what would become the most severe post-war recession up to that time.

The public sector does not have a monopoly on regrettable forecasts, and such projections are not limited to the realm of business cycle analysis. Private sector forecasts of interest rates are notoriously inaccurate. For example, one group of widely-read, long-time forecasters concluded in March 1989, after a detailed analysis of the preconditions for an interest rate peak, that both "[s]hort- and long-term interest rates will continue to rise."[3]

In mid-April 1989, a large investment banking firm wrote: Everyone . . . is eager for a peak in interest rates, and this only creates dynamics that make such a development improbable in the U.S. this year. Some additional moderate upward interest rate pressure still seems likely before the year is out (50-100 basis points from present levels across the yield curve).[4]

As Figure 1 illustrates, these forecasts were published as interest rates reached a peak and began to decline. Rather than increasing beyond the peak of 9.85 percent, registered on March 21, 1989, the yield on the one-year Treasury note fell to an average of 8.44 percent in June and to 7.53 percent in early December.[5]

Forecast accuracy is widely acknowledged to decrease with the length of the forecast horizon. That analysts encounter difficulty in recognizing fundamental changes even as they occur may be less well appreciated.[6] The above cases are striking examples.

Still, the record is not one-sided. The contributors to the ambitious 1968 publication, *The Five-Year Outlook for Interest Rates*, correctly forecasted that interest rates would still be high by historical standards in 1973.[7] The one-year Treasury note yield climbed from an average of 5.69 percent in 1968 to a monthly high of 8.82 percent in 1973.

More recently, a nationwide brokerage firm boldly and correctly predicted in late 1988 that a large reduction in long term interest rates would occur in early 1989.[8] The company took the unusual step of airing television commercials and running full-page newspaper advertisements to announce the forecast. Interest rates climbed for a brief period after the campaign, but ultimately declined substantially.

As encouraging as these success stories might be to would-be forecasters, neither truly reflects the state of the art. The unique *Five-Year Outlook for Interest Rates* combined extensive analyses by four leading economists. The group included one of the foremost authorities on the history of interest rates and two former members of the President's Council of Economic Advisors. One contributor later became a Governor of the Federal Reserve System.

The group's effort would be difficult to reproduce regularly. Even if it could be replicated on occasion, asset-liability managers do not typically enjoy access to such resources. With respect to the brokerage firm's forecast, there is also no assurance of a repeat performance. In fact, a more thorough review of interest rate forecasts suggests that all four examples are exceptions to the rule.

THE RECORD OF THE EXPERTS

The accuracy of most forecasters most of the time is mediocre. The best outperform the rest for only some variables and only during some periods. Even then, the margin of difference is usually thin. At the other extreme, even the worst forecasters produce adequate predictions on occasion.[9] From a review of interest rate predictions compiled as part of the American Statistical Association-National

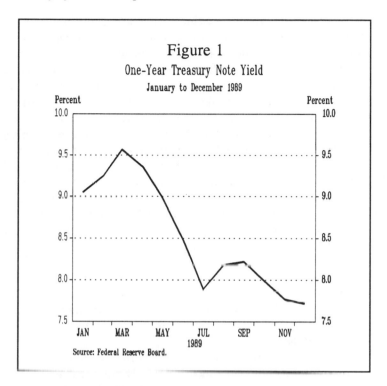

Figure 1
One-Year Treasury Note Yield
January to December 1989

Source: Federal Reserve Board.

Bureau of Economic Research (ASA-NBER) forecast surveys, Zarnowitz concluded that

> . . . no single forecaster has been observed to earn a long record of superior overall accuracy, and indeed nothing in the present study would encourage us to expect any individual to reach this elusive goal.[10]

The literature confirms that the standard of performance for economic forecasts falls well short of pinpoint accuracy. One study found that revisions to forecasts made during the year being forecast as often as not reduced accuracy, even with as much as six months of additional information.[11]

Several researchers have examined the interest rate forecasts published in the Goldsmith-Nagan *Bond and Money Market Letter*. The point predictions for selected interest rates three and six months hence have been compiled each quarter since September 1969 from a panel of approximately fifty experts. Three studies report mean absolute errors (MAE) of six-month ahead forecasts of the yield on the three-month Treasury bill of 68, 147, and 160 basis points.[12] The second two calculations are more representative of the panel's forecasting ability, because the first was calculated from a short sample period, during which interest rates were relatively stable.

Another study examined the forecasts of nine economists surveyed on a regular basis and over a comparable time period by the *Wall Street Journal* and found a MAE of 155 to 163 basis points.[13] Still another researcher found that predictions by major commercial forecasting firms of the three-month Treasury bill yield six months in the future were as far as 200 basis points away from the actual levels two-thirds of the time.[14] A projection of 7 percent, for example, would imply only a 67 percent chance that the actual value will lie between 5 percent and 9 percent.

Moreover, forecasters have done a poor job of predicting merely the direction of change, let alone the magnitude. The Goldsmith-Nagan forecasters ". . . consistently missed turning points . . . by 3 months in the case of the 3-month forecasts and by 6 months in the 6-month forecasts."[15]

The *Wall Street Journal* panel correctly anticipated the direction of change in the three-month Treasury Bill yield six months in advance less than half of the time.[16] Among the National Association of Business Economists and two nationwide economic consulting firms during the mid-1970s, ". . . there was almost a complete inability to anticipate major changes in the direction of rates; turning point errors were pronounced."[17]

BENCHMARK MEASURES

As poor as the experts' record of absolute accuracy may appear, it is not by itself sufficient evidence to label interest rate forecasts useless. The size and characteristics of errors do not by themselves determine the value of a forecast. A truer test is the value of the decisions to which it leads.

A quantitative assessment of the profitability of interest rate forecasts would require the measurement and analysis of the costs and benefits from producing and using the forecasts.[18] Such a detailed investigation lies outside the scope of this research. An indirect approach to gauging the usefulness of a forecast is to compare its performance with the records of benchmark projections. Forecast users must routinely question

> . . . whether there is strong evidence that the benefits in terms of increased forecast accuracy outweigh the costs, given the alternative of using low-cost, mechanical methods of prediction.[19]

The Naive Approach

The most basic method for producing benchmark forecasts is the naive, no-change model. Essentially costless to apply, the no-change model assumes that the level of interest rates in a future period will be the same as the level prevailing at the time the forecast is made.

On balance, research indicates that the performance of the experts compares favorably with, but does not outdistance the record of the no-change model. The MAE of the six-month ahead no-change forecasts of the three-month Treasury bill yield over the June 1982 to December 1986 period was 132 basis points. The forecasts from the *Wall Street Journal* panel had MAEs 15 to 20 percent higher.[20] From March 1977 to October 1987, the accuracy of the no-change predictions over three- and six-month horizons was comparable to the record of the Goldsmith-Nagan survey forecasts. The respective MAEs were not statistically distinguishable.[21] The inescapable conclusion is that experts' forecasts have not been significantly better than naive projections.[22]

Expectations and the Term Structure

The yield curve provides the raw material for a more rigorous, but still mechanical, calculation of interest rate forecasts. Irving Fisher was among the first to explicitly postulate that the term structure of interest rates contains information on investors' expectations about future levels of rates.[23] The term structure, of course, is the relationship among yields on debt instruments that differ only in term to maturity.

Since Fisher, others have modified and empirically tested the view that the spread between the yields of two instruments with different maturities incorporates an interest rate forecast. Following

Hicks, the "implied forward rate" for the one-year Treasury note one year hence, for example, is:

$$(1) \qquad r_{1,1} \;=\; \frac{(1 + r_2)^2}{(1 + r_1)} - 1 \;,$$

where r_1 and r_2 are the prevailing spot rates on the one-year and two-year Treasury notes, respectively.[24]

A numerical example is instructive. Assume that an investor with funds to commit for two years can choose between a one-year Treasury note yielding 5.5 percent and a two-year note yielding 6.0 percent. The investor has two alternatives. He can purchase a single two-year note or two successive one-year notes.

By the formula above, the implied forward rate for the one-year note in one year is 6.5 percent. Over the two-year investment horizon, the return from purchasing two one-year notes yielding 5.5 percent and 6.5 percent, respectively, will approximately equal the return from the two-year note with a 6.0 percent yield.

Other considerations aside, if the investor believes that the one-year yield will be higher than 6.5 percent in one year, he will opt for the strategy of buying two successive one-year notes. If he believes that it will be lower than 6.5 percent, he will purchase the two-year note.

Suppose he believes it will be higher. If enough other investors agree with him, their collective action will force the current price of the one-year note higher, lowering its yield. As the yield on the one-year note falls, the implied forward rate for the one-year note in one year rises, provided the current yield on the two-year note does not change.

Investors will continue to favor the purchase of the one-year note over the two-year note until the implied forward rate rises to the level that is expected to prevail in one year. As a result, according to the expectations theory, arbitrage will keep the many forward rates that are implicit in the yield curve in alignment with investors' expectations of future rate levels.[25]

In addition to expectations about future levels of spot rates, forward rates also incorporate liquidity premiums. These components rise with maturity to compensate investors for the greater price volatility of longer term securities. Moreover, liquidity premiums fluctuate with the level of yields, partially obscuring the forecasts that are imbedded in forward rates.[26] The result is that implied forward rates exceed expected rates by a variable amount.

The existence of liquidity premiums is easily established. If expectations are for rising rates as often as for falling rates, the expectations theory implies that short term rates should equal long term rates on average. In fact, the average of the yield on the one-year Treasury note from April 1953 to December 1989 was 6.23 percent, compared with an average of 6.79 percent for the ten-year note during the same period.[27] A more direct and conclusive observation is that, over a long span, the three-month and six-month forward rates exceeded the corresponding future spot rates by statistically significant margins.[28] In both cases, the difference is presumably accounted for by the liquidity premium.

Although controversy remains, forward rates do appear to reflect the market's perceptions of future spot rate levels. Moreover, when adjusted for the variation in premiums, forward rates have been shown to contain useful information about future interest rate levels.[29] Such research notwithstanding, the errors of forward rate forecasts are large in absolute terms.

One study found root mean squared errors (RMSE) of 96 and 143 basis points for forward rate predictions of three-and six-month Treasury bill yields, three and six months hence over the January 1966 to July 1976 period.[30] The RMSEs of the Goldsmith-Nagan and *Wall Street Journal* survey forecasts cited earlier ranged from 83 to 206 basis points, with all but one greater than or equal to 186 basis points.[31]

The differences in sample periods across most studies prohibit definitive conclusions. At least one study, however, has directly compared the Goldsmith-Nagan survey forecasts with premium-adjusted forward rates. The researcher concluded that the survey forecasts made more efficient use of available information than did the forward rates.

Survey forecasts of three-month Treasury bill yields six months in advance were shown to outperform the forward rate projections by a statistically significant margin, albeit the absolute difference was small.[32] In contrast, another study showed that the Goldsmith-Nagan forecasts of six interest rates over three- and six-month horizons were in some, but not all cases biased and ineffi-cient.[33]

Expectations and the Futures Market

Comparisons of survey forecasts with the implicit predictions of Treasury bill futures contracts are also inconclusive.[34] Just as in the case of premium-adjusted forward rates, the rates on futures contracts are rational in the sense that they provide unbiased estimates of future spot rates.[35] Futures forecasts neither over-predict nor under-predict consistently.

A very recent study of the comparative forecasting performance of futures and forward rates showed that the accuracy of forward rates and futures rates ninety-one days ahead was close over the 1977 to 1987 period. The futures rate forecast was found to be ". . . generally, but not universally superior to the forward rate forecast."[36]

The interaction of supply and demand for futures contracts provides a gauge of market expectations of future interest rate levels. Rates on futures contracts theoretically reflect all of the information available to investors regarding the future course of interest rates. As a result, futures rates might be expected to perform as well or better than the experts.

In terms of direction-of-change accuracy over a six month horizon, futures rates proved superior to the *Wall Street Journal* surveys.[37] With respect to point accuracy, the *Wall Street Journal* forecasts under-performed futures forecasts by some measures, but outperformed by others. Futures rate point forecasts performed better than the Goldsmith-Nagan panelists and the no-change model, but the difference between futures rate and survey forecasts was not statistically significant.[38]

THE STUMBLING BLOCK
OF MARKET EFFICIENCY

The similarity in the performance of forecasts from experts, market expectations, and naive methods seriously questions whether the sequential filter can make a meaningful contribution to interest rate forecasting. The efficient markets hypothesis states that all relevant information available at a given time is fully reflected in prices at that moment. As new information surfaces, prices and yields in spot and futures markets adjust immediately. Analysts can match, but not consistently exceed the accuracy of market-based forecasts.[39]

The efficient markets hypothesis places interest rate forecasts in a new light. "A useful forecast is not simply an accurate one; it also must tell something about the future that is not already reflected in current market interest rates."[40]

In practice, the record of expert and market-based interest rate forecasts is consistent with the theory. The performances of point forecasts from all sources lie within a narrow range. Even statistically significant differences are small, while the errors themselves are large in absolute terms.

The Forecaster's Paradox

Followed to its logical end, the efficient markets hypothesis leads to the forecaster's paradox. A rational forecaster in possession of relevant information unknown to anyone else would not share his forecast. He could increase his wealth by a greater margin through speculation in financial markets than through the sale of the forecast.

> As Ludwig von Mises used to point out to those who were tempted to succumb to the razzle-dazzle of economic forecasting: If someone were really able to forecast the economic future, he wouldn't be wasting his time putting out market letters or econometric models. He'd be busy making several trillion dollars forecasting stock and commodity markets.[41]

The implication is that any public forecast does not contain profitable information. Under such conditions, the appropriate reply to Einstein's question: "Where do you think interest rates will be in a year?" would be: "I don't know any more than what the futures market says, and if I did, I would not tell you!"

Grossman and Stiglitz argued that informationally efficient markets cannot exist.[42] But even if markets do operate efficiently, two important questions remain. Could circumstances exist under which a forecaster would share projections that he expects are more accurate on average than market-based predictions? And, could not incentives exist for users to purchase forecasts that they realize will be no more accurate than market-based predictions on average? To both questions, the answer is, "yes."

First, the probability of being right is not the only factor determining whether a forecaster will be willing to sell his forecast. His attitude toward risk-taking and the extent of his financial resources are also determining factors. For example, not everyone would make the trip to Las Vegas to gamble, even if they knew that on average they would "beat the house" 60 percent of the time. Some would be unwilling to risk a string of early losses that would erase their capital. Others might not have the required capital. On the other hand, many would be willing to place bets on behalf of someone else, in possession of the necessary appetite and resources, in exchange for a share of the proceeds.

Second, even market-based forecasts are not costless. The derivation of implied forward rates is ". . . both time consuming and costly . . . . [It] is a difficult task to do monthly, and expensive to do weekly or daily."[43] Some might argue that the advent of futures contracts on Treasury securities makes interest rate forecasting as easy as reading the financial section of the newspaper. Prices of interest rate futures contracts undeniably provide a valuable first step in the formulation of an interest rate outlook, but are not without drawbacks.

Futures rates provide explicit forecasts for only the four contract delivery dates each year.[44] In addition, the forecasts are strictly point estimates. Quotes on futures contracts do not provide any indication of the likelihood that the implied future spot rates will be observed. Are the distributions from which tomorrow's rates will be generated normal, skewed, compact, diffuse?

All of these questions have implications for the way the user will apply the forecast. To prudently act on an interest rate forecast, the asset-liability manager must know how much confidence to have in the projections. The issue of certainty can only be adequately addressed by statements about the probabilistic nature of the forecast. Such information is notably absent from market-based interest rate predictions.[45]

An additional consideration is the expected net marginal advantage of an expert forecast over a market-based forecast. The net marginal advantage is the difference between the cost of obtaining a forecast and the expected benefit from using it, less the difference between the cost and expected benefit from a market-based forecast. If the net difference is positive, then the purchase of the forecast makes economic sense.

Furthermore, gains may arise from specialization in comparative advantage—from forecasters specializing in producing predictions and end-users specializing in applying them. Even if a forecaster could apply his work more effectively than an end-user, or even if an end-user could forecast better than an analyst, their comparative advantages could be such that they both would gain by specializing in their area of expertise and pooling their talents by sharing the forecast.

The Fallacy of Omission

Finally, the apparent absence of a consistently superior forecaster is not proof of the efficient markets hypothesis. The fact that a preeminent prognosticator has not surfaced is weak support for the theory, at best. Indeed, the forecaster's paradox ensures that even if superior forecasts exist, they will not be observable. The paradox dooms the search for consistently market-beating performances.

Aside from the forecaster's paradox, the use of published forecasts to test the efficient markets hypothesis entails jointly testing the assumption that the particular survey chosen accurately reflects all forecasts.

A related point is crucial with respect to panel forecasts. Publicized predictions, especially those printed in such widely read circulars as the *Wall Street Journal*, may be aimed at goals other than accuracy. In a remarkable passage, Henry related that

> . . . many [Wall Street economists] believe little risk is attached to the day-to-day forecasting game. If you're hot, you'll get favorable publicity and so will your firm. And, during those periods when you're consistently wrong, so what. You'll surely have plenty of company, and being right or wrong doesn't seem to matter. One economist knows from repeated personal experience that nobody remembers what he has been quoted as having said—even as soon as one or two hours later, incredible as that may sound. But people do remember that you have been quoted, he says, and, after you appear in the press a few times, you become an authority figure in customers' minds.[46]

TOWARD A REDEFINITION OF THE PROBLEM

On balance, the evidence regarding the accuracy of interest rate forecasts suggests that the experts do not outperform market-based predictions with regularity. Although the experts do not under-perform, the absolute errors of forecasts from all sources are large. Clearly, there is room for improvement.

The forecaster's paradox explains why an outstanding forecaster will never emerge. It does not follow, however, that the preparation and application of forecasts cannot be improved. Indeed, the accuracy of both survey forecasts and econometric predictions has increased over time.[47] The accuracy of interest rate forecasts can be further enhanced, as new techniques are developed and applied.

The more efficient use of existing information also holds promise. Examples from outside financial markets are compelling. For instance, productivity in oil extraction has risen dramatically from the earliest days. Even if exploration ceased, advances in technology or a more intensive application of available technology could boost production by facilitating a more efficient use of existing fields. Likewise, the fact that the forecasting ability of the National Weather Service is hampered by reliance on antiquated equipment and procedures emphasizes the contribution that technology makes to forecast accuracy.[48]

In some respects, the interest rate forecasting problem is similar. Even if a forecaster cannot regularly uncover information unknown to the market, he might be able to more efficiently process the existing information. Zarnowitz believes it ". . . highly probable that economic forecasting can be improved to some degree and that we are far from having reached the limits of this process."[49]

At a minimum, there is substantial room to improve decision-making that is based on forecasts. The first step is to focus on the probabilities associated with the timing of key events, rather than estimating precise levels.

NOTES

1. Quoted in David Ahlers and Josef Lakonishok, "A Study of Economists' Consensus Forecasts," *Management Science* 29 (October 1983): 1113.

2. House Committee on Appropriations, *Testimony of Arthur Burns*, 93d Congress, 1st sess., 21 February 1974.

3. The Bank Credit Analyst, "Preconditions for an Interest Rate Peak," *Investment and Business Forecast* 40 (March 1989): 3.

4. Robert M. Giordano, "Interest Rate Outlook," *The Pocket Chartroom* (Goldman Sachs Economic Research Group), no. 4 (April 1989): C5.

5. All of the interest rates on federal government debt instruments used in this study are the "constant maturity" yields calculated by the Federal Reserve Board. The original sources for all interest rates are the Federal Reserve Board Statistical Releases H.15 and G.13, but the actual data used in this study were retrieved from The WEFA Group computer database. For a brief explanation of constant maturity yields, see Federal Reserve Board, "Selected Interest Rates," Federal Reserve Statistical Release G.13, no. 12 (5 December 1989): 2.

6. For evidence that accuracy declines with the forecast horizon, see Steven K. McNees, "How Accurate Are Macroeconomic Forecasts?" Federal Reserve Bank of Boston *New England Economic Review* (July/August 1988): 25, Victor Zarnowitz and Geoffrey H. Moore, "Sequential Signals of Recession and Recovery," *Journal of Business* 55 (January 1982): 57, and Victor Zarnowitz "Rational Expectations and Macroeconomic Forecasts," National Bureau of Economic Research, working paper no. 1070 (January 1983). Richard B. Worley and Stanley Diller, "Interpreting the Yield Curve," (Goldman Sachs Economics Research Report), (September 1976): 9 discovered the same phenomenon in implied forward rate forecasts calculated from the Treasury yield curve. For evidence of the poor record of identifying turning points, see Geoffrey H. Moore, *Business Cycles, Inflation, and Forecasting* (New York: National Bureau of Economic Research, 1983): 407, Herman O. Stekler, "An Evaluation of Quarterly Judgmental Economic Forecasts," *Journal of Business* 41 (July 1968), and Rendigs Fels and C. Elton Hinshaw, *Forecasting and*

Recognizing Business Cycle Turning Points (New York: National Bureau of Economic Research, 1968).

7. Herbert V. Prochnow, ed., *The Five-Year Outlook for Interest Rates* (Chicago: Rand McNally and Company, 1968).

8. "Gap Management Eases Interest Rate Swings," *Savings Institutions* 109 (Novemver 198): 44 and pamela Sebastian, "Predictor's Peril: Short One Recession, Wall Street Economist Hits a Bumpy Stretch," *Wall Street Journal* (New York) 30 October 1989, sec. A, p. 1.

9. McNees, "How Accurate Are Macroeconomic Forecasts?" 26.

10. Victor Zarnowitz, "The Accuracy of Individual and Group Forecasts from Business Outlook Surveys," *Journal of Forecasting* 3 (January/March 1984): 24.

11. Steven Strongin and Paula S. Binkley, "A Policymakers' Guide to Economic Forecasts," Federal Reserve Bank of Chicago *Economic Perspectives* 12 (May/June): 3.

12. The mean absolute error (MAE) is a standard measure of forecast accuracy and is calculated as:

$$MAE = \sum_{i=1}^{n} \frac{|F_i - A_i|}{n} ,$$

where F_i and A_i are the forecast and actual values of the *i-th* observation, respectively, and n is the total number of observations. The MAE is expressed in the same units as the variable being forecast (in this case, basis points) and indicates the amount by which the forecast is incorrect on average, without consideration of the direction of the error. The three MAE calculations are from Michael J. Prell, "How Well Do the Experts Forecast Interest Rates?" Federal Reserve Bank of Kansas City *Monthly Review* 58 (September/October 1973): 7, Pami Dua, "Multiperiod Forecasts of Interest Rates," *Journal of Business and Economic Statistics* 6 (July 1988): 382, and R. W. Hafer and Scott E. Hein, "Comparing Futures and Survey Forecasts of Near-Term Treasury Bill Rates," Federal Reserve Bank of St. Louis *Review* 71 (May/June 1989): 37.

13. Michael T. Belongia, "Predicting Interest Rates: A Comparison of Professional and Market-Based Forecasts," Federal Reserve Bank of St. Louis *Review* 69 (March 1987): 13.

14. Steven K. McNees, "Forecasting Accuracy of Alternative Techniques: A Comparison of U.S. Macroeconomic Forecasts," *Journal of Business and Statistics* 4 (January 1986): 11.

15. Prell, "How Well Do the Experts Forecast?" 5.

16. Belongia, "Predicting Interest Rates," 12.

17. Donald R. Fraser,"On the Accuracy and Usefulness of Interest Rate Forecasts," *Business Economics* 12 (September 1977): 43.

18. This argument is generally attributed to Jacob Mincer and Victor Zarnowitz, "The Evaluation of Economic Forecasts," in *Economic Forecasts and Expectations: Analyses of Forecasting Behavior and Performance*, ed. Jacob Mincer (New York: National Bureau of Economic Research, 1969), 20, but has its roots in earlier work by Henri Theil, Milton Friedman, and Carl Christ. More recently, it has become the underlying justification for the use of naive benchmark forecasts in evaluating the relative accuracy of survey forecasts.

19. Prell, "How Well Do the Experts Forecast?" 9.

20. Belongia, "Predicting Interest Rates," 13.

21. Hafer and Hein, "Comparing Futures and Survey Forecasts," 37.

22. Fraser, "On the Accuracy and Usefulness," 42.

23. Irving Fisher, "Appreciation and Interest," *Publications of the American Economic Association* 11 (August 1896): 23. The seeds of the expectations hypothesis appear in J. B. Say, *A Treatise on Political Economy* (Philadelphia: Lippincott, Grambo and Company, 1853), 343.

24. John R. Hicks, *Value and Capital* (London: Clarendon Press, 1939), 144-152.

25. As compelling as this argument may be, it has met with considerable resistance on both theoretical and empirical grounds. See Burton G. Malkiel, *The Term Structure of Interest Rates: Expectations and Behavior Patterns* (Princeton, New Jersey: Princeton University Press, 1966), 17-49 for a discussion of the evolution of the theory and the arguments of its detractors.

26. Benjamin M. Friedman, "Interest Rate Expectations Versus Forward Rates: Evidence From an Expectations Survey," *Journal of Finance* 34 (September 1979): 969.

27. The WEFA Group computer database.

28. Worley and Diller, "Interpreting the Yield Curve," 4.

29. Eugene F. Fama, "The Information in the Term Structure," *Journal of Financial Economics* 13 (December 1984): 509.

30. Worley and Diller, "Interpreting the Yield Curve," 9. Root mean squared error is similar to mean absolute error (RMSE) and is calculated as:

$$\text{RMSE} \;=\; \left[\sum_{i=1}^{n} \frac{(F_i - A_i)^2}{n} \right]^{1/2} ,$$

where F_i and A_i are the forecast and actual values of the i-th observation, respectively, and n is the total number of observations. The formula is from Dua, "Multiperiod Forecasts," 382.

31. Prell, "How Well Do the Experts Forecast?" 7; Dua, "Multiperiod Forecast," 382; Hafer and Hein, "Comparing Futures and Survey Forecast," 37; Belongia, "Predicting Interest Rates," 13.

32. Adrian W. Throop, "Interest Rate Forecasts and Market Efficiency," Federal Reserve Bank of San Francisco *Economic Review* (Spring 1981): 32.

33. Benjamin M. Friedman, "Survey Evidence on 'Rationality' of Interest Rate Expectations," *Journal of Monetary Economics* 6 (October 1980): 457-458, 460.

34. A futures contract is an agreement to purchase a specified quantity of a certain item at a predetermined price on a predetermined date. Trading in three-month Treasury bill futures has taken place at the Chicago Mercantile Exchange since January 6, 1976. Currently, six contracts are traded, with expirations of three, six, nine, twelve, fifteen, and eighteen months. For more information, see Albert Burger et al., "The Treasury Bill Futures Market and Market Expectations of Interest Rates," Federal Reserve Bank of St. Louis *Review* 59 (June 1977): 3 and Chicago Mercantile Exchange, *Opportunities in Interest Rates: Treasury Bill Futures*, 2d ed. (Chicago: Chicago Mercantile Exchange, 1979).

35. William Poole, "Using T-Bill Futures to Gauge Interest-Rate Expectations," Federal Reserve Bank of San Francisco *Economic Review* (spring 1978): 15 and Hafer and Hein, "Comparing Futures and Survey Forecasts," 39 found both futures and the Goldsmith-Nagan survey forecasts to be unbiased. Scott S. MacDonald and Scott E. Hein, "Futures Rates and Forward Rates as Predictors of Near-Term

Treasury Bill Rates," *Journal of Futures Markets* 9 (June 1989): 256 found futures to be unbiased and to contain no premium.

36. MacDonald and Hein, "Futures Rates and Forward Rates as Predictors," 253.

37. Belongia, "Predicting Interest Rates," 13.

38. Hafer and Hein, "Comparing Futures and Survey Forecasts," 37.

39. Oldrich A. Vasciek and John A. McQuown, "The Efficient Market Method," *Financial Analyst's Journal* 28 (September 1972): 75.

40. Belongia, "Predicting Interest Rates," 11.

41. Murray N. Rothbard, forward to *Economic Forecasting — Models or Markets?*, by Henry Fuller (San Francisco: Cato Institute, 1980): xii. A. Hamilton Bolton, *Money and Investment Profits* (Homewood, Illinois: Dow-Jones Irwin, 1967), 200-201 discusses the usefulness of the "perfect" stock market barometer.

42. Sanford S. Grossman and Joseph E. Stiglitz, "On the Impossibility of Informationally Efficient Markets," *American Economic Review* 70 (June 1980): 393.

43. Richard W. Lang and Robert H. Rasche, "A Comparison of Yields On Futures Contracts and Implied Forward Rates," *Federal Reserve Bank of St. Louis Review* 60 (December 1978): 23.

44. MacDonald and Hein, "Futures Rates and Forward Rates as Predictors," 260.

45. Stigum and Branch, *Managing Bank Assets*, 268.

46. George B. Henry, "Wall Street Economists: Are They Worth Their Salt?" *Business Economics* 24 (October 1989): 45.

47. In an analysis of the J. A. Livingston survey data from the Philadelphia Inquirer, Ahlers and Lakonishok, "A Study of Economists' Consensus Forecasts," 1124 found ". . . a substantial and gradual improvement in forecasting performance over time," even as economic fluctuations grew more erratic and presumably more difficult to forecast. McNees, "How Accurate Are Macroeconomic Forecasts," 25 noted improvement in forecasts of real GNP and the inflation rate over time. Hafer and Hein, "Comparing Futures and Survey Forecasts," 37 documented a substantial gain in accuracy in the prediction of the three-month Treasury bill yield; however, the decline in interest rate volatility over the course of the sample period could have accounted for all of the improvement.

48. Jerome Ellig, "For Better Weather, Privatize," *Wall Street Journal*, 4 December 1989, sec. A, p. 14.

49. Victor Zarnowitz, "The Record and Improvability of Economic Forecasting," reprint no. 880, National Bureau of Economic Research, Cambridge, Mass., June 1987, 14.

III
The Interest Rate Cycle

Historically, interest rates have followed a cyclical and repetitive pattern, with rates tending to trend in one direction for reasonably long periods of time.[1]

In many respects, the focus of financial markets is very short-term in nature. Securities traders can make or lose thousands of dollars due to the smallest of moves in prices. Therefore, traders speculate on the market's reaction to news scheduled for release in the next day or hour or even the next few minutes. Portfolio managers are charged with enhancing the value of assets under management over a longer stretch. Yet, the long run is inescapably a series of short runs, during which performance is judged by strict standards. Asset-liability managers face the reality that securities gains often boost reported profits today at the expense of a lower net interest margin tomorrow.

A greater ability to understand and anticipate movements in interest rates would help alleviate the conflict between short term pressures and long term objectives. The current state of interest rate forecasting is plainly not up to the task. Accuracy is uniformly poor. Predictions are usually point estimates, devoid of probabilistic content. Turning points are simply ignored or are defined by the direction of change over brief periods, often as short as one month.

The record suggests that there is ample room to improve short term point forecasts. Still greater gains, however, may be achieved by addressing a more relevant and attainable goal: the anticipation and recognition of cyclical turning points. A prerequisite is the definition and identification of the interest rate cycle. The business cycle studies of the National Bureau of Economic Research (NBER) provide a starting place.

ELEMENTS OF A CYCLE

Arthur Burns and Wesley Mitchell launched the modern era of business cycle analysis with their 1927 publication, *Business Cycles: The Problem and Its Setting*.[2] Since then, the accumulation of additional data and enhancements in statistical techniques have fostered a rich body of research on the business cycle. Economic theory and empirical analysis link business cycle forces and interest rates. Therefore, the work of Burns and Mitchell provides a basis for defining the interest rate cycle and establishing the dates of peaks and troughs.

The working definition, used at the NBER for over sixty years, describes the business cycle as that

> phenomenon consisting . . . of expansions occurring at about the same time in many economic activities, followed by similarly general recessions, contractions, and revivals which merge into the expansion phase of the next cycle; the sequence of changes is recurrent but not periodic; in duration business cycles vary from more than one year to ten or twelve years . . . .[3]

A full cycle spans the period between troughs, encompassing both an upswing and a downswing, and is readily distinguishable from other regular patterns in economic activity. Three key characteristics of a business cycle are the breadth, duration, and size of fluctuations in economic activity. Breadth refers to the proportion of economic indicators that exhibit cyclical co-movement. Duration is the calendar length of a cycle. Size refers to the degree of change.

Other Major Moves

Seasonal cycles are less broadly based than business cycles and, by definition, last for precisely one year. The length of a business cycle has no strict limits; however, shifts large enough to qualify as full cycles have not unfolded within a single year. In practice, all complete cycles have lasted for at least one year, with most stretching to four or more years. Finally, aggregate measures of activity change by smaller amounts over seasonal cycles than over business cycles.[4]

Secular movements are manifest as successively higher or lower peaks and troughs over a series of cycles. Also referred to as the trend, secular movements reflect the tendency of a time series to climb or fall during a period spanning more than one cycle.

Lastly, irregular fluctuations result from one-time events, such as natural disasters, shifts in government policies, or the exertion of market power by a cartel or labor union, for example. While special events may influence the timing of a business cycle turning point, they are distinct from cyclical forces. By definition, irregular fluctuations are nonrecurring, not pervasive, do not last long, and are often not large.

The moderation in the business cycle after World War II led to the related concept of the growth cycle.[5] A growth cycle is characterized by a pronounced decline in the rate of growth of the economy, not a decrease in its size. A business cycle can contain more than one growth cycle, and growth cycles are more narrowly based.

"I Know One When I See One"

The process used by the NBER to assign cyclical peaks and troughs begins with the identification of turning points in a large number of economic time series.[6] Cyclical turning points for the economy as a whole are then defined by the ". . . predominance of agreement in timing among specific cycles."[7]

In other words, clusters of turning points in individual measures of economic activity mark the neighborhoods of peaks and troughs in the business cycle. The specific business cycle reference dates are identified by further analysis, which includes judgments by members of the NBER business cycle dating committee.

Shooting in the Dark

Despite extensive research into the nature, causes, consequences, and forecasting of business cycles, no widely recognized definition of a turning point exists. Wecker followed others by adopting an expeditious description of business cycle peaks, but acknowledged that the turning point concept has ". . . not yet been fully refined . . . . Future research in this area will benefit from an economically meaningful and precise definition of a turning point."[8]

Recognizing the necessity of clearly defining the business cycle, Stock and Watson advanced a more precise description of a peak in economic activity. A Stock-Watson peak occurs in the month prior to the first of six significant and consecutive monthly declines in the NBER's coincident economic index. In practice, a decline is considered significant if it is larger than the value of a random variable used to represent the judgment of the NBER dating committee.[9] Despite the contribution of Stock and Watson, we are still without a rigorous and universally applicable definition of a turning point.

WHAT IS THE INTEREST RATE CYCLE?

In some ways, examination of the interest rate cycle is more straightforward than analysis of the business cycle. First, all interest rates are expressed in percent, which precludes the difficulties associated with converting disparate measures of economic activity to the same units.

Second, there is tighter co-movement among interest rates than among different economic statistics. For example, fluctuations in Aaa corporate bond yields and the federal funds rate over the interest rate cycle are more synchronized than are railroad car loadings and semiconductor shipments over the course of the business cycle. The high degree of co-movement among interest rates associated with credit instruments of different maturity and quality is illustrated in Figure 2.

The principles of business cycle analysis lead to a working definition:

> The interest rate cycle is the element, which is common to all interest rates, that is manifest as the co-movement among yields on financial instruments of different credit quality and term to maturity. A full cycle extends from peak to peak or from trough to trough. A half cycle extends from peak to trough or from trough to peak. The interest rate cycle is not limited in duration and does not require a specific quantitative change in yields. Nonetheless, the interest rate cycle is characterized by agreement in the direction of change in the predominance of individual yields.

THE COMPOSITE INTEREST RATE CYCLE INDEX

Burns and Mitchell determined reference dates by examining the cyclical peaks and troughs in hundreds of individual series. The

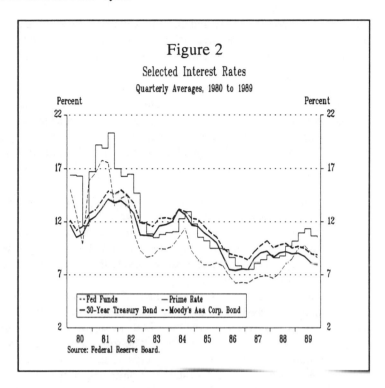

Figure 2

Selected Interest Rates

Quarterly Averages, 1980 to 1989

Percent   Percent

Legend:
- -- Fed Funds
- — Prime Rate
- — 30-Year Treasury Bond
- -- Moody's Aaa Corp. Bond

80 81 82 83 84 85 86 87 88 89

Source: Federal Reserve Board.

months around which the individual series' turning points clustered were identified as turning points in overall economic activity. The homogeneity among interest rates permits the calculation of a single index to represent the state of interest rates and serve as the basis for identifying turning points in the interest rate cycle. One advantage of such an approach is that the turning points of a single series can be identified more concretely than can the "predominance of agreement" among a number of individual series.

Construction of the Index

The Composite Interest Rate Cycle Index (CIRCI) is constructed from the yields on six separate financial instruments that differ in credit quality and term to maturity. The six component rates are the yields on (1) the three-month Treasury bill, (2) 180-day commercial paper, (3) the one-year Treasury note, (4) the five-year Treasury note,

(5) the ten-year Treasury note, and (6) Moody's composite index of corporate bond yields. Beyond diversification of credit quality and term to maturity, the criteria for selection included the availability of the data from the early 1950s forward.

The use of a composite index, as opposed to a specific, individual yield, to represent the interest rate cycle has both drawbacks and advantages. The reliance on a single interest rate, such as the yield on the one-year Treasury note, for example, would have the advantage of using directly observable data. In addition, the analyst could address the specific question: "Is a turning point in the one-year Treasury yield near?"

The data transformations involved in calculating the CIRCI are a shortcoming. Data manipulation risks masking valuable information in the original series. The transformations could also create seemingly significant fluctuations when none truly exist. Nonetheless, a composite index more closely simulates the interest rate cycle than could the yield on any one particular instrument.

The interest rate cycle is like the path of a satellite orbiting the earth. Scientists use a system of tracking stations around the globe to gather data on the location of the satellite, from which they can calculate its precise trajectory and position. The interest rate cycle can be viewed similarly, with the readings on yields of an array of financial instruments serving the role of the satellite monitoring stations.

The application of modern statistical methods, such as state-space and VAR modeling, might do a better job of tuning in the signal from the selection of interest rates than the method used and described below, but the use of a composite index is probably a better proxy for the interest rate cycle than a single rate.

The CIRCI is compiled using a modified version of the methodology developed at the NBER and employed by the U.S. Department of Commerce to calculate the composite indexes of leading, coincident, and lagging indicators.[10] The CIRCI is calculated through a three-step process: standardization, reverse trend adjustment, and index cumulation.

The chief difficulty in combining the six interest rates into a single index is that short term rates are more volatile than long term rates. Therefore, the first step is to standardize the fluctuations in each interest rate.

Standardization. The standardization procedure begins with the calculation of the month-to-month percent changes for each component interest rate. The percent changes are computed using the symmetrical percent change formula introduced by Shiskin in 1961.[11] The formula is still used by the Commerce Department in the calculation of its composite indexes to avoid the distortions that result from the conventional formula for computing percent changes. The percent change, C_t, of a series, X_t, is typically calculated as:

$$(2) \qquad C_t = \frac{100 \ (X_t - X_{t-1})}{X_{t-1}} \ .$$

For series that include frequent and large increases and decreases, such as interest rates, the familiar formula yields distorted measures of percent change.

Consider a series that alternates in value between 5 and 10. Despite the fact that the value changes by the same amount each period, the conventionally calculated percent change oscillates substantially, from 100 percent to -50 percent. In contrast, the symmetrical formula, which expresses the percent change as:

$$(3) \qquad C_t = \frac{200 \ (X_t - X_{t-1})}{X_t + X_{t-1}}$$

yields a uniform 66.67 percent change for the constant unit change. Although X has no trend, the conventional formula would yield an average percent increase of 25 percent, whereas the symmetrical formula appropriately calculates an average percent change of zero.

The month-to-month percent changes in the shorter term interest rates are larger in absolute value than the percent changes for the longer term interest rates, and would therefore dominate the index. To equalize the impact of all six component interest rates on the final index, the raw month-to-month percent changes of each rate are divided by a standardization factor unique to that rate.

The standardization factor for a particular interest rate is the average of the absolute values of the symmetrical percent changes over the entire sample period, May 1953 to December 1989. The standardization factor for series X, is computed as:

$$(4) \qquad F_x = \sum_{i=1}^{n} \frac{|X_t|}{n} \, ,$$

where X_t is the symmetrical percent change in series X during period t and n is the number of observations in the sample.

The standardization process forces the average over the sample period of the absolute values of the symmetrical percent changes to equal one. The standardization factors for the six component interest rates are listed in Table 1. As expected, standardization factors vary inversely with maturity.

Trend elimination. The second step involves the removal of the trend from the average of the symmetrical percent changes of the six component interest rates. The Commerce Department adjusts the percent changes in the leading, coincident, and lagging composite indexes in such a way that the average of the month-to-month percent changes in each index over the sample period is equal to the estimated long term growth rate of the economy.

The trend is removed from the CIRCI because the long term trend in interest rates is theoretically zero.[12] Rates are conceptually more akin to the growth rate than to the size of the economy. Economic growth tends to rise and fall around some natural value. The size of the economy increases almost monotonically.

To eliminate the trend, the average of the standardized percent changes of the six component rates are first cumulated into a preliminary index with the base month of April 1953 equal to 100. The trend of the resulting series is estimated as the 75-term centered moving average of the preliminary index.[13] The missing 37 values at the beginning and end of the moving average are extrapolated, using the rate of change between the moving average values for the first and last months and the moving average values two years later and earlier, respectively. The trend is removed by subtracting the moving average from the preliminary index and adding 100 to the result.

Index cumulation. In the final step, the trend-adjusted preliminary index is converted back into month-to-month percent changes and accumulated into an index. The average of the index values

Table 1
STANDARDIZATION FACTORS FOR THE
COMPOSITE INTEREST RATE CYCLE INDEX
MAY 1953 TO DECEMBER 1989

Interest Rate	Standardization Factor
3-Month Treasury Bill	5.59417
180-Day Commercial Paper	4.67525
1-Year Treasury Note	5.10542
5-Year Treasury Note	3.44954
10 Year Treasury Note	2.64860
Corporate Bond (Moody's Composite)	1.45156

Source: Data from the Federal Reserve Board and
calculations by the author.

during the base period of January to December 1989 is set equal to the average of the observed annual values of the six component series during the year. A desirable consequence is that the CIRCI is expressed in terms of "1989 percent" throughout the 1953-1989 period.

The resulting index is shown in Figure 3. The trend adjustment process has the effect of visually emphasizing the cycle, without—in nearly all cases—altering the selection of turning point dates.[14] The scaling to 1989 percent facilitates comparison across cycles.

Identification of Peaks and Troughs

If the interest rate cycle coincided closely with the business cycle and had the same period, the process of identifying peaks and troughs in interest rates would be trivial. In reality, cycles in interest rates and business activity are related, but are not identical.

This research could perhaps have been conducted with interest rate turning point dates selected in accordance with business cycle reference dates with no harm to the conclusions. As Cagan observed, however, ". . .[i]nterest rates appear to reflect special influences more

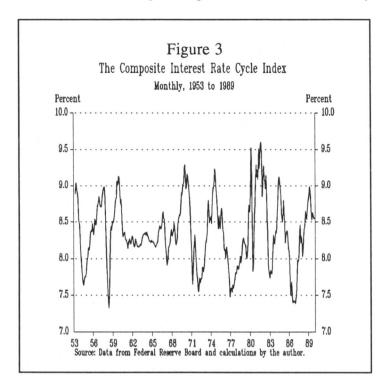

Figure 3
The Composite Interest Rate Cycle Index
Monthly, 1953 to 1989

Source: Data from Federal Reserve Board and calculations by the author.

often than price and output series do."[15] As a result, a strict adherence to business cycle reference dates would artificially and unnecessarily limit the number of meaningful cyclical fluctuations for study.

In search of a method. Analysis of the interest rate cycle is different from analysis of the business cycle in two important ways. First, since business expansions are longer and larger than business contractions, the secular trend in economic activity is upward. The result is that the economy expands over time. The natural tendency of the economy to grow stems from population growth and increases in productivity. In contrast, periods of secular increases or decreases in interest rates are eventually followed by periods of offsetting movements.[16]

Consequently, interest rates do not display an inherent tendency to rise or fall, albeit rates have increased or decreased on balance for periods as long as several decades. To wit, the world economy is many, many times larger today than it was two and a half millennia ago, yet the rate on short term credit was as low as 8 percent to 8.33 percent in Greece and Rome circa 400 B.C., compared with 8.25 percent (for federal funds) in the United States today.[17]

Second, interest rates undergo more frequent periods of pronounced decline than does the economy.[18] As a consequence, the interest rate cycle more closely resembles the economic growth cycle than the business cycle. Figure 4 shows the yield on the three-month Treasury bill from 1946 to 1989. The vertical lines designate the NBER business cycle reference dates. While large swings in interest rates do coincide with cyclical fluctuations in overall economic activity, they also occur on occasion within half cycles.

The growth cycle agrees more closely, but still not perfectly, with the large swings in the three-month Treasury bill yield.[19] For example, interest rates underwent at least two full cycles during the single December 1978 to December 1982 economic growth cycle. In contrast, rates showed little cyclical movement during the growth cycles of the 1940s. Neither the business cycle nor the growth cycle offers an easy solution to the problem of dating interest rate peaks and troughs.

Moore faced a similar problem in deriving reference dates for the inflation cycle.[20] He used a computer program developed by NBER researchers, which employs the criteria used by the Bureau in dating business cycles.[21] The program has been shown to essentially duplicate the NBER business cycle reference dates in an objective and mechanical fashion. Moore found, however, that it failed to select sizable, but short-lived fluctuations in inflation and (more frequently) selected fluctuations that lasted for a long time, but were not sufficiently large. Although the date selections of the program were generally satisfactory, Moore made judgmental alterations in several instances.

Interest rates usually change markedly over the course of the interest rate cycle, but may also undergo large fluctuations that are not cycle-related. Use of the NBER computer algorithm or a strict size-and-duration rule for identifying turning points poses a problem. Both are prone to select reference dates that do not correspond to shifts in cyclical factors. Any big change in rates has implications for asset-liability management, but cyclical movements are more readily anticipated than other fluctuations.

The guiding light of monetary policy. The Federal Reserve discount rate reflects factors that influence the general level of market

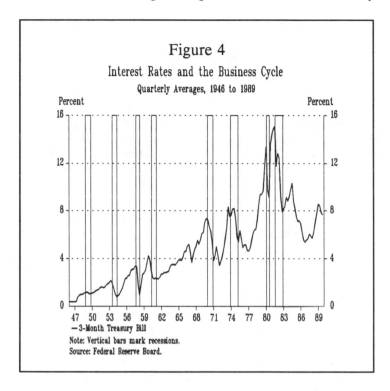

Figure 4

Interest Rates and the Business Cycle

Quarterly Averages, 1946 to 1989

— 3-Month Treasury Bill

Note: Vertical bars mark recessions.

Source: Federal Reserve Board.

interest rates.[22] Consequently, the initial decline ". . . in the discount rate following several months or even years of hikes is fairly safe confirmation that an interest-rate peak has been seen."[23] Since the Federal Reserve Board administers the discount rate in accordance with developments in financial markets, shifts usually occur after changes in credit market fundamentals have already affected market interest rates.[24] Nonetheless, a direction reversal serves as a first round identifier of interest rate cycle turning points by indicating that a peak or trough has just occurred or is about to occur.

A cycle timing system based on changes of direction in the discount rate might be less consistent than a computer-based method. The criteria of a computer-based system can be held constant over a long period. In contrast, the "reaction function" of the Federal Reserve Board (that is, the Federal Reserve's formal and informal system of interpreting events and formulating policy responses) shifts over time with changes in the Board's composition and the political climate.[25]

The discount rate method is more objective in the sense that the conclusions of all researchers would be the same. Different researchers would tend choose different criteria for a computer-based algorithm or a size-and-duration selection method.

An additional and important advantage of the discount rate rule is the timeliness with which it confirms tentatively identified turning points. The median lag from a turning point to a discount rate reversal over the 1953-1989 period was 4.0 months. In contrast, the NBER will not assign a date to a turning point in the business cycle until at least six months have passed. The lag has often been longer.

Even the computer-based procedure used to identify growth cycles requires a long lag between the occurrence and recognition of turning points. The program relies on trend calculations that are subject to large revisions for the most recent several years of the time series.[26]

Selection rules and results. The dates of peaks and troughs in the interest rate cycle were selected by the following rules. First, a change in the discount rate that is in the opposite direction of the immediately preceding change indicates that a turning point has occurred in the interest rate cycle. Second, the date of a turning point is that month—prior to the discount rate change, but no earlier than the month of the previous turning point—during which the CIRCI assumed its highest or lowest value.

Third, turning points can occur no more frequently than every three months. Interest rate moves that last less than three months are probably not sufficiently large or diffuse to qualify as cycles. In practice, the three-month limit is moot. The CIRCI has not changed sharply enough over any two-month span for the shift to be classified as a half cycle.

Figure 5 shows the CIRCI from April 1953 to December 1989. The hollow vertical bars represent periods of declining interest rates. The left edges mark troughs and the right edges mark peaks. Table 2 lists the dates of direction reversals in the discount rate and the corresponding dates of turning points in the interest rate cycle.

Two peaks are omitted from the table and much of the following analysis. The discount rate changed direction in February 1954, designating June 1953 as a peak. The decrease in the CIRCI over the last nine months of 1989 was large enough to tentatively identify

March as a peak. The CIRCI fell 44 basis points, or 5.0 symmetrical
percent, from March to December 1989.

The June 1953 peak is discarded because values of the CIRCI
begin only two months earlier, severely limiting the test of the
sequential filter. The March 1989 peak is discarded because the
discount rate has not yet confirmed the month as a turning point by
reversing course. In addition, the omission of the last peak provides for
an out-of-sample test of the sequential filter.

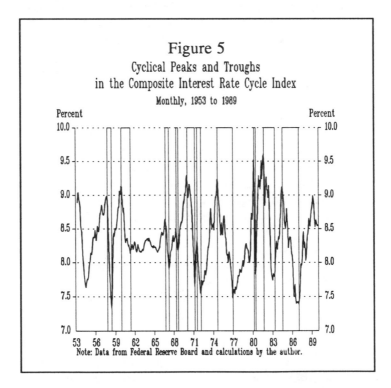

Figure 5
Cyclical Peaks and Troughs
in the Composite Interest Rate Cycle Index
Monthly, 1953 to 1989

Note: Data from Federal Reserve Board and calculations by the author.

The turning points chosen by the discount rate rule probably
conform closely to the judgment of most analysts. The March to June
1980 half cycle might be considered too short or not the result of
cyclical forces. The May to September 1968 and March to July 1971
half cycles are susceptible to the same criticisms.

Table 2
CYCLICAL PEAKS AND TROUGHS IN THE
COMPOSITE INTEREST RATE CYCLE INDEX (CIRCI)
1954 TO 1988

Dates of Half Cycles Trough to Peak	Date of Discount Rate Reversal	Length of Half Cycle in months	Change in CIRCI in basis points	Change in CIRCI in percent[a]
7/54 - 10/57	4/55	39	134	16.1
6/58 - 12/59	9/58	18	180	21.9
5/61 - 9/66	7/63	64	50	6.0
4/67 - 5/68	11/67	13	58	7.1
9/68 - 1/70	12/68	16	110	16.0
3/71 - 7/71	7/71	4	67	8.4
2/72 - 8/74	1/73	30	168	20.0
12/76 - 3/80	8/77	39	204	24.0
6/80 - 9/81	9/80	15	177	20.3
5/83 - 7/84	4/84	14	132	15.6
Average		**25.2**	**128**	**15.5**

Dates of Half Cycles Peak to Trough				
10/57 - 6/58	11/57	8	-165	-20.2
12/59 - 5/61	6/60	17	-99	-11.5
9/66 - 4/67	4/67	7	-73	-8.8
5/68 - 9/68	8/68	4	-30	-3.6
1/70 - 3/71	10/70	14	-164	-19.4
7/71 - 2/72	11/71	7	-77	-9.7
8/74 - 12/76	12/74	28	-175	-20.9
3/80 - 6/80	5/80	3	-169	-19.5
9/81 - 5/83	11/81	20	-180	-20.7
7/84 - 1/87	11/84	30	-173	-21.0
Average		**13.8**	**-131**	**-15.5**

a Symmetrical percent change.
Source: Data from the Federal Reserve Board and calculations
      by the author.

Excluding the June 1953 and March 1989 turning points, ten peaks and ten troughs were selected using the above criteria. The CIRCI underwent nine peak-to-peak and nine trough-to-trough cycles during the period. In contrast, the 1953-1989 period contained six full peak-to-peak business cycles, not including the current expansion. Eight complete growth cycles occurred, not including the growth recovery from 1986 to 1989.

Peak-to-trough half cycles, or downturn regimes, lasted an average of 13.8 months over the October 1957 to January 1987 period. The longest was the most recent confirmed downturn regime from July 1984 to January 1987, which lasted 30 months. The shortest was the three-month half cycle from March to June 1980.

Trough-to-peak half cycles, or upturn regimes, have been nearly twice as long as downturn regimes, lasting 25.2 months on average over the July 1954 to July 1984 period. Even without the unusually long May 1961 to September 1966 episode, upturn regimes lasted an average of nearly 21 months. Upturn regimes lasted as long as 64 months and were as short as four months. Even though the CIRCI is adjusted to have no trend, the interest rate cycle was in an upturn regime in 252 of 390 months, or 64.6 percent of the time.

As a result of the trend-adjustment process, the average degree of change in the CIRCI was almost identical during upturn and downturn regimes. The CIRCI decreased by an average of 131 basis points (in 1989 percent) during downturn regimes and increased by an average of 128 basis points during upturn regimes. The average symmetrical percent change was -15.5 percent during downturn regimes and 15.5 percent during upturn regimes.

The largest half cycle decline in the CIRCI was 180 basis points from September 1981 to May 1983. The average was 174 basis points in the four most recent downturn regimes. The largest half cycle increase was 204 basis points from December 1976 to March 1980, compared with an average of 170 basis points during the four most recent upturn regimes. The symmetrical percent changes ranged from a 3.6 percent decrease to a 24.0 percent increase.

Birds of a Feather

The data transformations involved in the calculation of the CIRCI risk introducing errors. In practice, any such effects should be insignificant. Unlike most other statistical forecasting techniques, the sequential filter does not operate directly on the values of a time series. Instead, the sequential filter uses only the dates of turning points and observations on an indicator series, which are not transformed.

Table 3 shows that the timing of turning points in the six component series do not differ substantially from the timing of turning points in the CIRCI. The left column lists the dates of peaks and troughs in the composite index. Each line shows the number (1-6) of components that turned in the same month as the CIRCI and in each of the thirteen months before and after. For example, at the January 1987 trough, three of the component series turned in the same month as the CIRCI, two turned three months before the CIRCI, and the sixth turned two months after. The bottom line shows the totals for each month.

Figure 6 shows that 56.8 percent of the turns in component series occurred in the same month as the turn in the CIRCI. An additional 24.2 percent occurred either one month before or after, so that 81.1 percent of all turns in component rates occurred within one month of the turn in the CIRCI. Nearly 90 percent occurred within two months. Moreover, the turns in the index before detrending corresponded almost exactly with the turns in the final CIRCI. The two exceptions were one-month differences at the September 1968 trough and the July 1984 peak. The detrending process delayed the turning point in each case.

The dispersion of component series turning points around the CIRCI turns was very small. The timing of turning points in the non-detrended and the detrended CIRCI were almost identical. Accordingly, neither the use of a composite index nor the trend removal process distorted the selection of turning point dates.

SUMMARY

Developed in accordance with business cycle theory, the composite interest rate cycle index is intended as a proxy for that element common to all interest rates called the interest rate cycle. The discount rate rule is a useful means of identifying shifts from one regime to another, and the resulting turning points are closely related to, but not uniform with the economic growth cycle.

Table 3a
CLUSTER ANALYSIS OF TROUGH TURNING POINTS IN
THE CIRCI AND ITS SIX COMPONENTS
1953 TO 1988

Type and Date of Trough Turning Point	Month from Trough Turning Point[a]																										
	-13	-12	-11	-10	-9	-8	-7	-6	-5	-4	-3	-2	-1	0	1	2	3	4	5	6	7	8	9	10	11	12	13
7/54	.	.	.	.	.	.	.	.	.	.	.	1	2	1	.	.	.	.	2	.	.	.	.	.	.	.	.
6/58	.	.	.	.	.	.	.	.	.	.	.	1	1	3	1	.	.	.	.	.	.	.	.	.	.	.	.
5/61	.	.	.	.	.	.	.	.	.	2	.	1	.	2	1	.	.	.	.	.	.	.	.	.	.	.	.
4/67	.	.	.	.	.	.	.	.	.	.	.	.	1	3	.	2	.	.	.	.	.	.	.	.	.	.	.
9/68	.	.	.	.	.	.	.	.	.	.	.	.	3	2	.	1	.	.	.	.	.	.	.	.	.	.	.
3/71	.	.	.	.	.	.	.	.	.	.	.	.	.	6	.	.	.	.	.	.	.	.	.	.	.	.	.
2/72	.	.	.	.	.	.	.	.	.	.	.	1	1	3	.	.	.	.	.	.	.	1	.	.	.	.	.
12/76	.	.	.	.	.	.	.	.	.	.	.	.	.	5	.	.	.	.	.	.	.	.	1	.	.	.	.
6/80	.	.	.	.	.	.	.	.	.	.	.	.	.	6	.	.	.	.	.	.	.	.	.	.	.	.	.
5/83	.	.	.	.	.	.	1	.	1	.	.	.	1	3	.	.	.	.	.	.	.	.	.	.	.	.	.
1/87	.	.	.	.	.	.	.	.	.	.	2	.	.	3	.	1	.	.	.	.	.	.	.	1	.	.	.
Total	.	.	.	.	.	.	1	.	1	2	2	4	9	37	2	4	.	.	2	.	.	1	1	1	.	.	.

a For each row, month zero corresponds to the date of the trough in the CIRCI listed in the leftmost column. The values in each row are the number of components that reached a trough in the month at the top of each column.

Source: Calculations by the author.

Table 3b

CLUSTER ANALYSIS OF PEAK TURNING POINTS IN
THE CIRCI AND ITS SIX COMPONENTS
1953 TO 1988

Type and Date of Peak Turning Point	Month from Peak Turning Point[a]																										
	-13	-12	-11	-10	-9	-8	-7	-6	-5	-4	-3	-2	-1	0	1	2	3	4	5	6	7	8	9	10	11	12	13
6/53												1	1	3	1	1											
10/57													1	4	1												
12/59														4	2												
9/66													1	4			1										
5/68														4	2												
1/70													2	2													
7/71														6						1							
8/74													1	3		1											1
3/80														6													
9/81													4	4	1			1									
7/84													4	1	1												
Total												1	14	38	7	2	1	1		1							1

a For each row, month zero corresponds to the date of the peak in the CIRCI listed in the leftmost column. The values in each row are the number of components that reached a peak in the month at the top of each column.

Source: Calculations by the author.

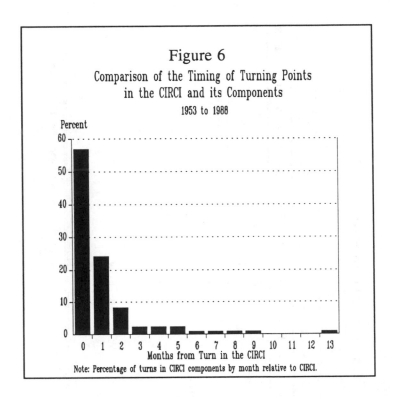

Figure 6

Comparison of the Timing of Turning Points
in the CIRCI and its Components

1953 to 1988

Note: Percentage of turns in CIRCI components by month relative to CIRCI.

The size and duration of interest rate cycles and half cycles vary within a broad range. As evidenced by a cluster analysis of turning points in the CIRCI and its six components, interest rate cycles are widely diffused and consistent in timing across different instruments.

NOTES

1. Paul H. Wilson, "Can Interest Rates Really Be Predicted?" *Pension World* 23 (May 1987): 18.

2. Arthur F. Burns and Wesley C. Mitchell, *Business Cycles: The Problem and Its Setting* (New York: National Bureau of Economic Research, 1927).

3. Arthur F. Burns and Wesley C. Mitchell, *Measuring Business Cycles* (New York: National Bureau of Economic Research, 1946): 1.

4. Geoffrey H. Moore and Victor Zarnowitz, "The Development and Role of the National Bureau of Economic Research's Business Cycle Chronologies," in *The American Business Cycle: Continuity and Change*, ed. Robert J. Gordon (Chicago and London: University of Chicago Press, 1986), 736.

5. Ilse Mintz, "Dating United States Growth Cycles," *Explorations in Economic Research* 1 (summer 1974): 1.

6. Approximately 95 percent of the 830 monthly and quarterly time series originally examined by Mitchell displayed specific cycles. Wesley C. Mitchell, *Business Cycles and Their Causes* (Berkeley: University of California Press, 1941), 10.

7. Mitchell, *Business Cycles*, 10.

8. William E. Wecker, "Predicting the Turning Points of a Time Series," *Journal of Business* 52 (January 1979): 50.

9. From Mark W. Watson, "The New Leading Indicators and Recession Index," (presentation to the Fourth Federal Reserve District Economic Roundtable, Cleveland, Ohio, January 26, 1990). For a comprehensive discussion of Stock and Watson's research, see James H. Stock and Mark W. Watson, "New Indexes of Coincident and Leading Economic Indicators," in *NBER Macroeconomics Annual 1989*, ed. Oliver Jean Blanchard and Stanley Fischer (Cambridge, Massachusetts: The MIT Press, 1989), 351.

10. For a detailed description of the methodology behind the construction of the Commerce Department's composite indexes, see Ronald A. Ratti, "A Descriptive Analysis of Economic Indicators," *Federal Reserve Bank of St. Louis Review* 67 (January 1985): 14; U.S. Department of Commerce, *The Handbook of Cyclical Indicators* (Washington, D.C.: U.S. Government Printing Office, 1984), 65; and

Marie P. Hertzberg and Barry A. Beckman, "Business Cycle Indicators: Revised Composite Indexes," *Business Conditions Digest* 29 (January 1989): 97.

11. Julius Shiskin, "Signals of Recession and Recovery: An Experiment with Monthly Reporting," occasional paper no. 77, National Bureau of Economic Research, Cambridge, Mass., 1961, 123-124.

12. Phillip Cagan, "Changes in Cyclical Behavior of Interest Rates," occasional paper no. 100, National Bureau of Economic Research, Cambridge, Mass., 1969, 7 noted offsetting trends in long term rates and no well-defined trends in short term rates whatsoever.

13. Charlotte Boschan and Walter W. Ebanks, "Phase-Average Trend: A New Way of Measuring Economic Growth," in *Proceedings of the Business and Statistics Section* (washington, D.C.: American Statistical Association, 1978), 333.

14. Cagan, "Changes in the Cyclical Behavior," 8 concluded that the trend in interest rates played no part in changes across business cycles in the timing of interest rate turning pointts relative to business cycle reference dates.

15. Cagan, "Changes in the Cyclical Behavior," 3.

16. Sidney Homer, *A History of Interest Rates*, 2d ed. (New Brunswick, New Jersey: Rutgers University Press, 1977), 43, 56.

17. Homer, *A History of Interest Rates*, 43, 56.

18. Cagan, "Changes in the Cyclical Behavior," 3.

19. Moore and Zarnowitz, "The Development and Role," 774.

20. Geoffrey H. Moore, *Business Cycles, Inflation, and Forecasting* (New York: National Bureau of Economic Research, 1983), 178. The problem faced by Moore was more tractable because the inflation cycle is more closely correlated with the economic growth cycle than is the interest rate cycle. See Geoffrey H. Moore, "Five Little-known Facts about Inflation," in ibid., 171.

21. For a description of the methodology behind the computer program, see Charlotte Boschan and Gerhard Bry, "Cyclical Analysis of Time Series: Selected Procedures and Computer Programs," technicnal paper no. 20, National Bureau of Economic Research, Cambridge, Mass., 1971.

22. Daniel L. Thornton, "The Discount Rate and Market Interest Rates: What's the Connection?" Federal Reserve Bank of St. Louis *Review* 64 (June/July 1982), 3.

23. Martin Pring, *How To Forecast Interest Rates* (New York: McGraw-Hill Book Company, 1981), 170.

24. William C. Melton, *Inside the Fed: Making Monetary Policy* (Homewood, Illinois: Dow-Jones Irwin, 1985), 132.

25. Steven K. McNees, "Modelling the Fed: A Forward-Looking Monetary Policy Reaction Function," Federal Reserve Bank of Boston *New England Economic Review* (November/December 1986), 3-4, 7.

26. Boshcan and Ebanks, "The Phase-Average Trend," 334. Mintz, "Dating United States Growth Cycles," 13.

IV
Benchmark Turning Point Forecasts

A common way of appraising a set of forecasts is to compare the results with what could have been achieved by some simple method of extrapolation.[1]

The true test of a forecast is the quality of the decisions to which it leads. More precisely, the value of a forecast depends on the benefits from using it, compared with the cost of acquiring it. The comprehensive and accurate measurement of net benefits of a forecast is elusive in practice.[2] Yet, a continuous and rigorous review of the successes and failures of forecasts is a prerequisite for improvement.[3]

To facilitate the analysis and upgrading of economic projections, forecasters have typically compared their predictions with extrapolations produced from simple, objective models. The no-change assumption is the purest example of a naive forecast, and is widely used to establish a minimum standard of accuracy for interest rate forecasts. The no-change model always projects the level of interest rates to be the same at the end of the forecast period as at the time the forecast is made.

In the context of a turning point forecasting problem, however, the no-change model is meaningless. The target of turning point forecasts is the timing of an event, not the level of a specific time series. To fill the void, two naive models for forecasting turning points in the interest rate cycle are derived and applied. Two other rules are developed to assess the prevailing state of interest rates. The four models establish a standard of accuracy against which sequential filter turning point forecasts can be judged.

THE NAIVE FILTER

The definition of the interest rate cycle, itself, provides a basic and effective benchmark for other forecasting methods. The discount rate reversal rule is the turning point analog of the naive no-change model. It simulates the potential performance of a forecaster who is armed only with an understanding of how the interest rate cycle is identified. Any forecasting method with merit should handily outperform the discount rate rule.

A prime rate rule is a natural extension of the discount rate rule. Changes in the prime rate often occur on expectations of changes in the discount rate. More frequently, the prime is adjusted in response to changes in monetary policy that appear first in other actions of the Federal Reserve. As a result, a prime rate rule should have a longer lead time than the discount rate rule.

The speculative nature of a prime rate rule may also result in false signals. A false signal is a warning of a turning point that does not materialize. Of course, since the interest rate cycle is defined in terms of the discount rate, a discount rate rule will generate no false signals.

TUNING IN THE SIGNAL

Specifically, a turning point signal is defined to occur when an indicator time series, Z, assumes a non-zero value according to the rule:[4]

$$(5) \qquad Z_t = \begin{cases} 1 \text{ if a trough occurred at time t,} \\ -1 \text{ if a peak occurred at time t,} \\ 0 \text{ otherwise.} \end{cases}$$

In turn,

(6) $\qquad Z_t = S_t - S_{t-1}$

where S_t is the value of the time series, S, which represents the state of interest rates at time t. The time series, S, describes whether rates are in an upturn or downturn regime. The state of interest rates at time t is defined as:

(7) $\qquad Z_t = \begin{cases} 0 \text{ if } X_t < X_{t-1} \text{ or } S_{t-1} = 0, \\ 1 \text{ if } X_t > X_{t-1} \text{ or } S_{t-1} = 1, \end{cases}$

where X_t, for $t = 1, 2, \ldots, n$, are the observed values of an indicator series, X. In this case, X is either the discount rate or the prime rate.

Table 4 provides a simple example. The indicator series, X, classifies interest rates to be in a downturn regime when $S_t - 0$, which in the sample case is for $2 <= t <= 3$ and $t => 7$. Interest rates are indicated to be in an upturn regime when $S_t = 1$, which is for $4 <= t <= 6$ in the example. The naive filter generates a trough turning point signal at $t = 4$, when $Z_t = 1$, and a peak turning point signal at $t = 7$, when $Z_t = -1$.

A standard of accuracy is established from the discount rate and prime rate rules by comparing the corresponding Z_t for $t = 1, 2, \ldots, n$ with the turning points in the CIRCI on two criteria. The first is the number of months remaining in half cycles on average after a turning point signal, expressed as a percent of the average length of the half cycles. The second is the size of the basis point move in the CIRCI from the date of a turning point signal to the end of the half cycle, expressed as a percent of the average basis point change over half cycles.

When a signal occurred prior to the turning point, the first measure was set to 100 percent, but the second measure was calculated in the same fashion as when the signal occurs after the turning point. The intent was to gauge the effects that the signals produced by the naive filters of the discount rate and prime rate time series would have had on investment results.[5]

SCORING THE BENCHMARK FORECASTS

Tables 5 and 6 show the key accuracy measures of the CIRCI turning point forecasts generated by the discount rate and prime rate rules, respectively. The top half of each table refers to troughs and the ensuing upturn regimes. The bottom half refers to peaks and the sub-

Table 4
AN EXAMPLE OF TURNING POINT
SIGNAL DETECTION

t	X_t	S_t	Z_t
1	3	n.m.	n.m.
2	2	0	0
3	2	0	0
4	3	1	1
5	4	1	0
6	4	1	0
7	3	0	-1
8	2	0	0
9	1	0	0

n.m. Not meaningful.
Source: Author's example.

subsequent downturn regimes. The first column lists the dates of the half cycles—trough to peak in the case of upturn regimes and peak to trough in the case of downturn regimes. The second column lists the dates of the turning point signals that correspond to the first dates listed in the first column. The third column shows the lead (-) or lag (+) of signals in months.

In Table 6, column four lists the number and length of false signals that occurred during the half cycle leading up to the corresponding turning point. For example, Table 6 shows that the prime rate rule produced a trough signal in May 1977, five months the actual trough

Table 5a
ACCURACY OF DISCOUNT RATE TROUGH
TURNING POINT FORECASTS
JULY 1954 TO JANUARY 1987

Dates of Half Cycles Trough to Peak	Date of Trough Signal	Lead (-)/ Lag (+) in months	Length of Half Cycle After Signal		Change in CIRCI After Signal	
			in months	% of half cycle	in basis points	% of total change
7/54 - 10/57	4/55	+9	30	76.9	84	62.7
6/58 - 12/59	9/58	+3	15	83.3	77	42.8
5/61 - 9/66	7/63	+26	38	59.4	36	72.0
4/67 - 5/68	11/67	+7	6	46.2	13	22.4
9/68 - 1/70	12/68	+3	13	81.3	82	74.5
3/71 - 7/71	7/71	+4	0	0.0	0	0.0
2/72 - 8/74	1/73	+11	19	63.3	126	75.0
12/76 - 3/80	8/77	+8	31	79.5	183	89.7
6/80 - 9/81	9/80	+3	12	80.0	102	57.6
5/83 - 7/84	4/84	+11	3	21.4	37	28.0
Average		+8.5	16.7	66.3	74	57.8*

a Average basis point change after signal as a percent of average basis point change over entire half cycle.
Source: Data from the Federal Reserve Board and calculations by the author.

Table 5b
ACCURACY OF DISCOUNT RATE PEAK
TURNING POINT FORECASTS
JULY 1954 TO JANUARY 1987

Dates of Half Cycles Peak to Trough	Date of Peak Signal	Lead (-)/ Lag (+) in months	Length of Half Cycle After Signal		Change in CIRCI After Signal	
			in months	% of half cycle	in basis points	% of total change
10/57 - 6/58	11/57	+1	7	87.5	-165	90.3
12/59 - 5/61	6/60	+6	11	64.7	-41	41.4
9/66 - 4/67	4/67	+7	0	0.0	0	0.0
5/68 - 9/68	8/68	+3	1	25.0	-1	3.3
1/70 - 3/71	10/70	+9	5	35.7	-112	68.3
7/71 - 2/72	11/71	+4	3	42.9	-22	28.6
8/74 - 12/76	12/74	+4	24	85.7	-131	74.9
3/80 - 6/80	5/80	+2	1	33.3	-35	20.7
9/81 - 5/83	11/81	+2	18	90.0	-105	58.3
7/84 - 1/87	11/84	+4	26	86.7	-123	71.1
Average		+4.2	9.6	69.6	-72	55.1[a]

a Average basis point change after signal as a percent of average basis point change over entire half cycle.
Source: Data from the Federal Reserve Board and calculations by the author.

Table 6a

ACCURACY OF PRIME RATE TROUGH
TURNING POINT FORECASTS
JULY 1954 TO JANUARY 1987

Dates of Half Cycles Trough to Peak	Date of Trough Signal	Lead (-)/ Lag (+) in months	False Signals: number/ duration in months	Length of Half Cycle After Signal		Change in CIRCI After Signal	
				in months	% of half cycle	in basis points	% of total change
7/54 - 10/57	3/54	-4		39	100.0	100	74.6
6/58 - 12/59	9/58	+3		15	83.3	77	42.8
5/61 - 9/66	12/65	+55		9	14.1	30	60.0
4/67 - 5/68	11/67	+7		6	46.2	13	22.4
9/68 - 1/70	11/68	+2		14	87.5	100	90.9
3/71 - 7/71	5/71	+2		2	50.0	25	37.3
2/72 - 8/74	4/72	+2		28	93.3	149	88.7
12/76 - 3/80	5/77	+5	2/6	34	87.2	151	74.0
6/80 - 9/81	9/80	+3		12	80.0	102	57.6
5/83 - 7/84	8/83	+3	1/1	11	78.6	61	46.2
Average		+7.8	3/7	17.0	67.3	81	63.1*

a Average basis point change after signal as a percent of average basis point change over entire half cycle.
Source: Data from the Federal Reserve Board and calculations by the author.

Table 6b
ACCURACY OF PRIME RATE PEAK
TURNING POINT FORECASTS
JULY 1954 TO JANUARY 1987

Dates of Half Cycles Peak to Trough	Date of Peak Signal	Lead (-)/ Lag (+) in months	False Signals: number/ duration in months	Length of Half Cycle After Signal		Change in CIRCI After Signal	
				in months	% of half cycle	in basis points	% of total change
10/57 - 6/58	1/58	+3		5	62.5	-37	22.4
12/59 - 5/61	8/60	+8	1/8	9	52.9	-16	16.2
9/66 - 4/67	1/67	+4		3	42.9	-19	26.0
5/68 - 9/68	9/68	+4	1/1	0	0.0	0	0.0
1/70 - 3/71	3/70	+2		12	85.7	-131	79.9
7/71 - 2/72	10/71	+3		4	57.1	-36	46.8
8/74 - 12/76	10/74	+2	1/5	26	92.9	-119	68.0
3/80 - 6/80	5/80	+2	4/20	1	33.3	-88	52.1
9/81 - 5/83	9/81	0	1/4	20	100.0	-141	78.3
7/84 - 1/87	9/84	+2		28	93.3	-159	91.9
Average		+2.9	8/38	10.8	78.3	-75	57.2*

a Average basis point change after signal as a percent of average basis point change over entire half cycle.

Source: Data from the Federal Reserve Board and calculations by the author.

in December 1976. The table also shows that the prime rate rule produced two false trough signals. The errant warnings lasted for a total of six months during the period of falling rates that preceded the December 1976 to March 1980 upturn regime.

The last four columns of each table present the accuracy measures of the benchmark turning point forecasts. The portion of the half cycle that occurred after the signal is listed in months and as a percent of the length of the half cycle, in separate columns. The portion of the change in the CIRCI over the half cycle that occurred after the signal is shown in basis points and as a percent of the total change in the CIRCI during the half cycle in the last two columns.

The changes in the CIRCI remaining in each half cycle after the signals reflects the impact of false warnings. The basis point changes in the CIRCI that occurred during false signal episodes are subtracted from the moves that took place after correct signals. As a consequence, the summary measures reflect the impacts that the signals from the naive filters could have had on investment decisions.

As expected, discount rate signals lagged at all turning points. On average, peak signals came 4.2 months after the actual peaks. Trough signals occurred an average of 8.5 months after the actual troughs. Excluding the protracted May to September 1966 half cycle, the average lag at troughs was 6.6 months. Apparently, the Federal Reserve has adjusted the highly visible and politically sensitive discount rate more quickly when interest rates have begun to fall than when rates have begun to rise.

During the typical regime, the discount rate signal occurred with approximately two-thirds of the half cycle remaining. On average, 66.3 percent of upturn regimes elapsed after trough signals. An average of 69.6 percent of downturn regimes elapsed after peak signals. On two occasions, during one downturn and one upturn regime, the signal coincided with the last month of the half cycle.

Nonetheless, the discount rate rule signaled switches from falling to rising rates with an average of 74 basis points remaining in the upturn regime. In relative terms, an average of 57.8 percent of the increase in the CIRCI occurred after the signal. The performance was similar at peaks. The rule signaled switches from rising to falling rates with an average of 72 basis points remaining in the downturn regime, or 55.1 percent of the average decrease.

Also as expected, the prime rate rule was superior by all measures, albeit marginally. On average, the prime rate rule issued turning point signals 7.8 months and 2.9 months after troughs and peaks, respectively. Excluding the extremely long lag at the May 1961 turning point, the average lag at troughs was 2.6 months.

The adjusted lag at troughs is statistically indistinguishable from the lag at peaks. In other words, commercial banks appear to have changed the prime rate no more quickly when rates have begun to rise than when rates have begun to fall. This finding contrasts with the popular view that banks are quicker to raise than to lower lending rates.

The prime rate signal led the interest rate cycle only once, at the July 1954 trough. At both troughs and peaks, the prime rate signal occurred with more time remaining in the subsequent half cycle than did the discount rate signal. Accordingly, the average basis point moves after prime rate signals were larger than after discount rate signals.

The naive filters of the discount rate and prime rate establish accuracy benchmarks for forecasts of turning points in the interest rate cycle. These benchmarks can be used to judge the performance of sequential filter turning point forecasts.

A BROADER SCOPE

The comparison of the predicted with the actual state of interest rates for all months provides another dimension to the standard of accuracy and facilitates the testing of two additional forecasting rules.[6]

Economic theory supports the view that implied forward rates contain a market-based forecast of interest rates, as well as a liquidity premium.[7] Using the yields on the six-month Treasury bill and one-year Treasury note, a forecast of the state of interest rates is determined by:

$$(8) \qquad S_t \;=\; \begin{cases} 0 \text{ if } r_t^6 > r_t^{6,6}, \\[2mm] 1 \text{ if } r_t^6 < r_t^{6,6}, \end{cases}$$

where r_t^6 is the observed equivalent bond yield on the six-month Treasury bill for month t and $r_{t6,6}$ is the forward rate at time t for the six-month Treasury bill six months hence.

Theory suggests that financial futures also contain interest rate forecasts. A second forecasting rule derives from the yields on three-month Treasury bill futures contracts. Specifically:

$$(9) \qquad S_t \;=\; \begin{cases} 0 \text{ if } r_t^3 > r_t^{3,6}, \\[2ex] 1 \text{ if } r_t^3 < r_t^{3,6}, \end{cases}$$

where r_t^3 is the monthly average of weekly observations on the three-month Treasury bill yield (discount basis) and $r_t^{3,6}$ is the monthly average of weekly observations on the futures contract on the three-month Treasury bill expiring in month $t+6$.[8]

Table 7 shows the percentage of months for the entire September 1954 to December 1988 period and for two sub-samples (to accommodate data limitations for implied forward and futures rates), during which each of four benchmark forecasting rules correctly indicated whether interest rates were in an upturn or downturn regime.

Table 7
STATE-OF-INTEREST-RATES FORECASTS
SEPTEMBER 1954 TO DECEMBER 1988

Naive Filter	Sample Period		
	9/54 - 12/88	1/59 - 12/88	3/77 - 12/88
Discount Rate	72.6	71.1	79.6
Prime Rate	68.0	66.7	81.7
Forward Rate	n.a.	40.6	48.6
Futures Rate	n.a.	n.a.	54.2

n.a. Not available.
Source: Data from the Federal Reserve Board and the *Wall Street Journal*
and calculations by the author.

Over the entire sample period, the discount rate rule correctly identified the state of interest rates 72.6 percent of the time. The prime rate rule outperformed the discount rate rule with respect specifically to turning points, but was inferior when all months were considered.

The prime rate rule identified the correct regime in only 68.0 percent of the months. Early and false signals lowered the score of the prime rate rule. The performances of the discount and prime rate rules changed little from the entire sample period to the 1959-1988 subsample.

Surprisingly, the naive filters of the discount and prime rate rules were far superior to the forward rate rule during the 1959-1988 period. As defined above, the Treasury forward rates correctly identified the state of interest rates only 40.6 percent of the time.

The accuracy of all three rules improved in the March 1977 to December 1988 period. The futures rate rule identified regimes with 54.2 percent accuracy. Futures rates outperformed forward rates by a modest margin, but significantly under-performed the discount and prime rate rules. The most interesting finding is that—according to the state-of-interest-rates criterion—the naive discount rate and prime rate rules were superior to the rules based on the more-theoretically-appealing implied forward and futures rates.

The turning point and state-of-interest-rates forecasts derived in this chapter will serve as benchmarks against which the sequential filter of the leading inflation index is judged.

NOTES

1. Geoffrey H. Moore, *Business Cycles, Inflation, and Forecasting* (New York: National Bureau of Economic Research, 1983), 413.

2. Zarnowitz, "The Record amd Improvability of Economic Forecasting," 2.

3. Moore, *Business Cycles*, 426.

4. This notation is derived from Wecker, "Predicting the Turning Points of a Time Series," 41.

5. A similar rule is used to gauge the usefulness of a leading inflation index in anticipating peaks an troughs in bond yields in John P. Cullity, "Signals of Movements in Inflation and Interest Rates," *Financial Analyst's Journal* 43 (September/October 1987): 47.

6. This test is suggested by James H. Stock and Mark W. Watson, "New Indexes of Coincident and Leading Economic Indicators," in *NBER Macroeconomics Annual 1989*, vol. 4, ed. Olivier Jean Blanchard and Stanley Fischer (Cambridge, Mass.: MIT Press, 1989), 382.

7. The forward rate is calculated from the equivalent bond yield of the secondary market discount rate on the six-month Treasury bill and the yield of the one-year Treasury note according to the formula in Richard B. Worley and Stanley Diller, "Interpreting the Yield Curve," research report, Goldman Sachs Economics, New York, 1976, 11.

8. The data are from the WEFA Group, Inc. financial computer database. In practice, the rate on the futures contract expired four, five, or six months from month t. As a consequence, the forecasts are based on a less than optimal application of the futures rates. The results therefore understate the predictive ability of futures rates.

V
Selecting a Leading Indicator

> . . . those of us who have worked in this field know that
> the thing that really makes high interest rates is inflation getting out
> of control . . .[1]

The first step in testing the ability of the sequential filter to forecast turning points in the interest rate cycle is the identification of the indicator to be filtered. A review of the factors affecting interest rates provides a starting point.

FACTORS AFFECTING INTEREST RATES

In recent years, both the press and the economic literature have suggested a large number of determinants of interest rates. Among the popular candidates are: the foreign exchange value of the dollar, the U.S. trade deficit, international capital flows, foreign interest rates, oil prices, the pace of domestic economic activity, the federal budget deficit, the tax structure, monetary policy, business capital spending, financial deregulation, market power of commercial banks, the savings and loan debacle, and even the maturing of the Baby Boom generation.[2] The extent to which these and other factors influence interest rates must be assessed within a theoretical framework.

The Wicksellian Theory of Loanable Funds

Writing at the turn of the century, the Swedish economist, Knut Wicksell, advanced the loanable funds theory of interest rates. Wicksell termed the rate of interest that equates the supply and demand for loanable funds the "natural interest rate." It depends, he said,

. . . on the efficiency of production, on the available amount of fixed
and liquid capital, on the supply of labour and land, in short on all
the thousand and one things which determine the current economic
position of a community; and with them it constantly fluctuates.[3]

At the core of the loanable funds theory is the idea that the
interest rate is the price of credit and is therefore determined by the
interaction of the supply and demand for credit. The desired real
investment curve (I) in Figure 7 illustrates the amount of loanable funds
demanded at different interest rates. The desired real saving curve (S)
shows the amount of funds supplied, or loaned, at different levels of
interest rates. The magnitudes R^e and Q^e are the equilibrium values of
the interest rate and the quantity of credit—the magnitudes that equate
intended real investment and saving.

The simple Keynesian saving function expresses saving as a
positive function of income (Y) and the accelerator principle states that
net investment is a positive function of the change in income.[4] Broadly
speaking, then, the natural rate of interest is a function of the level of
and change in national income.

The Gibson Paradox and the Fisher Effect

The apparent conflict of the loanable funds theory and classical
economic theory with empirical observation led to what Keynes named
the "Gibson Paradox."[5] Classical economic theory postulated an
inverse relationship between interest rates and economic activity and a
direct relationship between the pace of activity and the price level. Low
interest rates were required for strong economic activity. A strong
economy produced high prices. By association, low interest rates should
coexist with high prices. The paradox was that interest rates were in
fact highly positively correlated with commodity prices.

Irving Fisher addressed the apparent conundrum by hypothesiz-
ing that the observed rate of interest, the "nominal rate," has two
components. The first is a stable "real rate." The second is an inflation
premium equal to the expected future rate of change in the general
price level.[6] The relationship can be written:

(10) $rn_t = rr_t + pe_t$.

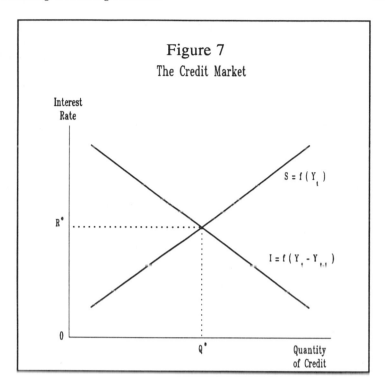

Figure 7
The Credit Market

Interest
Rate

$S = f(Y_t)$

R^*

$I = f(Y_t - Y_{t-1})$

0

Q^*

Quantity
of Credit

where rn_t is the nominal rate of interest at time t, rr_t is the real interest rate at time t, and pe_t is the expected rate of increase in prices over the maturity of the underlying asset as of time t. Also called the ex ante real rate, rr_t is the rate of interest expected to prevail after the anticipated change in the general level of prices. In contrast, the *ex post* real rate of interest is the nominal rate, rn_t, less the actual rate of inflation.

Fisher further assumed that the real rate changed only slowly over time. As a result, the real interest rate can be expressed as a constant, plus a random disturbance term with a mean of zero:[7]

(11) $$rr_t = rr + u_t.$$

The real rate is Wicksell's natural rate of interest and represents the marginal rate of return from holding real capital. It is the percent by which the total output of a society exceeds the corresponding costs of production.[8]

Imagine the extreme and narrow case of an economy in which the sole activity is the raising of cattle for slaughter. The natural rate of interest is the annual net increase in the number of head as a percent of the size of the herd at the beginning of the year, less the living expenses of the ranchers.

The inflation premium protects the real value of lenders' capital from erosion by the expected portion of inflation. The value of money varies inversely with the general level of prices, falling or rising in direct relation to the rate of inflation or deflation. The inflation premium compensates the lender for the expected decrease in the purchasing power of the dollars with which the loan will be repaid in the future.[9]

Fisher further postulated that expected inflation is a positive function of past rates of actual inflation:

$$(12) \qquad pe_t = \sum_{i=1}^{n} w_i \, pa_{t-i} \, ,$$

where pa_{t-i} is the actual rate of inflation i periods in the past, w_i is the weight with which the corresponding past rate of inflation affects expectations of future inflation, and n is the maximum lag of actual inflation that affects expectations.

Fisher further argued that the *ex ante* real rate is independent of both the actual and expected rates of inflation. As a result, an acceleration in prices will boost the expected rate of inflation, increase the inflation premium, and raise the nominal rate of interest. Termed the "Fisher Effect," this chain of events explains the positive correlation between the price level and the nominal rate of interest, demystifying the Gibson Paradox.

The Inflation-Interest Rate Link

Although Fisher provided the first statistical study of the issue, the observation of co-movement between inflation and interest rates dates back at least four thousand years.

> If a trader has lent wheat . . . at interest, then for every gur of wheat he shall take 100 qa as interest. If he has lent silver at interest, then for each shekel of silver he shall take a sixth part of a shekel, plus six grains, as interest.[10]

Somewhat more recently, William Douglass wrote in 1740 that inflationary expansions in the money supply ". . . rise the interest to make good the sinking principal."[11] In a speech before the House of Commons in 1811, Henry Thornton observed that someone who borrowed at 5 percent and repaid the loan after a period of 2 percent inflation, ". . . would find that he had borrowed at . . . 3 percent, and not at 5 percent as he appeared to do."[12] By at least 1981, the United States Congress acknowledged that "[t]he public simply will not hold securities unless yields exceed expected inflation."[13]

The notion that the expected rate of inflation influences the level of interest rates has withstood the rigors of economic theory, as well as the test of time.[14] Since Fisher, Cagan, Kessel and Alchian, Friedman, and others have explored and refined the theory behind the observation.[15]

The perception of an inflation-interest rate link has also survived modern statistical analysis. Using annual data from 1869-1963, Gibson tested the joint hypothesis that nominal interest rates reflect expected inflation and that expected inflation is based on past actual rates of inflation with affirmative results.[16] Using direct observations of anticipated inflation, Gibson later confirmed that expected inflation plays a key role in determining nominal interest rates[17] Keran and Zeldes provided indirect evidence of the linkage by showing that ". . . interest-rate differentials across countries reflect differences in inflation expectations."[18]

MEASURING THE THEORY

Even more notable than the existence of a connection between expected inflation and interest rates is the apparent strength of the relationship. Pigott implied that changes in inflation expectations are responsible for most of the variation in nominal interest rates.

> In the long-run . . . the real interest rate is mainly determined by the productivity of capital, which in turn reflects the savings decisions of

households, businesses, and government, the growth of the labor
force, and the rate of progress of technology. Generally these
conditions change slowly, so that the expected long-run real interest
rate . . . can be regarded as essentially constant when considering a
period of years.[19]

Fama concluded that virtually all of the variation in nominal
interest rates in the 1950s and 1960s was due to fluctuations in inflation
expectations.[20] Walsh found a dominant role for inflation expectations
in the 1960s and 1970s, but a secondary role in the first half of the
1980s.[21]

British capital markets offered direct evidence of the preemi-
nence of the inflation expectations effect on bond yields in the early to
mid-1980s. Britain began issuing bonds that are indexed to the British
retail price index (RPI) in 1982. At maturity, the holders of the
instruments will receive the original principal amount, plus a sum equal
to the change in the purchasing power of the principal, calculated from
the percent change in the RPI over the life of the bond.

As a result, the market yields are directly observable real
interest rates. Ranson showed that during a period of large swings in
nominal interest rates, the market yields of the indexed bonds remained
essentially unchanged. Apparently, changes in inflation expectations
caused nearly all of the changes in nominal yields.[22]

The Fisher Equations

Using variations of Fisher's equations, others have found
inflation expectations to have a less than absolute, but still dominant
influence on nominal interest rates. Pyle estimated that observed price
expectations alone accounted for 86 percent of the variation in nominal
yields from 1954 to 1969.[23] Lahiri calculated the impact over the
1952-1970 period at between 70 and 80 percent.[24] Feldstein and
Eckstein estimated a liquidity preference function, which revealed that
79 percent of the variation in the yield to maturity on Moody's Aaa
corporate bond yields from 1966 to 1969 was attributable to changes in
inflation expectations.[25]

The conclusion holds for the 1953-1989 period as well.
Substituting equations (11) and (12) into equation (10) leaves:

(13) $$rn_t = rr + \sum_{i=1}^{n} w_i\, pa_{t-i} + u_t \, ,$$

Equation (13) was estimated by ordinary least squares with quarterly data from the second quarter of 1953 through the fourth quarter of 1989. The nominal interest rate, rn_t, is the quarterly average of the constant maturity yield on the one-year Treasury note. The actual of inflation, pa_t, is the annualized rate of increase in the quarterly average of the seasonally adjusted consumer price index for all commodities.

Following Yohe and Karnosky, the model was estimated using the Almon lag technique.[26] The results are shown in Table 8. The R-squared indicates that past inflation rates explain approximately three-quarters of the variation in nominal interest rates during the 1953-1989 period. The coefficients of the distributed lags sum to unity, indicating, as Fisher suggested, that inflation expectations are ultimately fully reflected in nominal interest rates.

The t-values, in parentheses below the coefficients, indicate that the coefficients are statistically significant at the 1 percent level. The constant term suggests that the real one-year rate averaged approximately 2 percent during the period, which is consistent with widely held views regarding the level of real short term interest rates.

The Durbin-Watson statistic is too low to reject the null hypothesis of no first-order autocorrelation among the residuals. The autocorrelation may result from the omission of one or more variables that have significant effects on the nominal interest rate. Although the coefficients remain unbiased under such conditions, the R-squared may overstate the share of the variation in the one-year Treasury note yield attributable to changes in inflation expectations.

The Loanable Funds Model

In part to overcome this drawback, Sargent derived a reduced-form Wicksellian loanable funds model. The model incorporates the effects of real income and the real money supply on the nominal interest rate.[27] A major advantage of the specification is that it allows for a variable real interest rate.

The results from annual data for the period 1902-1940 corroborated earlier findings of a strong relationship between expected

Table 8
REGRESSION RESULTS FOR FISHER'S MODEL
SECOND QUARTER 1953 TO FOURTH QUARTER 1989

$$m_t = 1.97 + \sum_{i=1}^{20} w_i \, pa_i \, ,$$
$$(7.91)$$

where

$$\sum_{i=1}^{20} w_i = 1.00$$
$$(20.39)$$

$$R^2 = 0.74 \quad D\text{-}W = 0.27 \quad SE = 1.64$$

Key:
m = yield on one-year Treasury note.
pa = annualized percent change in the consumer price index.
w = weights with which past rates of inflation
      affect inflation expectations.

Source: Data from the Federal Reserve Board and the U.S. Department
of Commerce. Calculations by the author.

inflation and nominal interest rates. The diagnostic statistics suggest
that the approach mitigates the problems inherent in Fisher's equation.
Sargent concluded that

> . . . the most surprising aspect of the results is the extent of the
> contribution which the distributed lag price change variable makes to
> the explanation of variations in nominal yields after the other
> monetary and real variables have been taken into account.[28]

Yohe and Karnosky estimated Sargent's loanable funds model
with quarterly data for the 1961-1969 period. To measure the relative
importance of each of the independent variables, Yohe and Karnosky

calculated "beta" coefficients[29] Inflation expectations were the most important explanatory variable, having the greatest influence on nominal yields. In fact, the "beta" coefficient for price level changes was nearly three times as large as the second most important variable, real Gross National Product (GNP).

Estimation of Sargent's loanable funds model from 1959 to 1989 shows that inflation expectations have remained the dominant factor behind fluctuations in nominal interest rates. The regression results in Table 9 were calculated with quarterly data from the second quarter of 1959 to the fourth quarter of 1989. The nominal interest rate, rn_t, is the constant maturity yield on the one-year Treasury note. The level of real income, Y, is real GNP in 1982 dollars. The percent change in real money supply, M, is M2 in 1982 dollars. Actual inflation, pa, is the annualized rate of increase in the quarterly average of the consumer price index.

The sum of "beta" coefficients of the lagged actual inflation terms is .831—four and a half times larger than the combined "beta" coefficients of the real GNP variables and nearly three times larger than the real money supply variable. According to the above regression results, fluctuations in inflation expectations (as represented by the distributed lag of past actual rates of inflation) were the dominant factor determining movements in the one-year Treasury yield from 1959 to 1989.

Economic theory and empirical analysis suggest that leading indicators of inflation should contain information that is useful in efforts to forecast major swings in interest rates.

SELECTING A LEADING INDICATOR

The tendency of a time series, X, to lead another time series, Y, does not necessarily mean that X lends itself well to the process of anticipating turning points in Y. A leading indicator is useful in practice to the extent that it is: (1) available on a timely basis, (2) subject to few and/or small revisions, and (3) conducive to the extraction of signals.

Of course, the best leading indicators always generate signals in advance of actual turning points, do not issue extraneous signals, and have lead times with a small variance. In addition, the most trustworthy leading indicators are tied to the target series by economic theory.

Table 9
REGRESSION RESULTS FOR SARGENT'S MODEL
SECOND QUARTER 1959 TO FOURTH QUARTER 1989

$$m_t \;=\; \begin{array}{c} 1.7172 \\ (2.96) \end{array} - \begin{array}{c} 0.0046 \\ (0.94) \end{array} (Y_t - Y_{t-1})$$

$$+\; \begin{array}{c} 0.9677 \\ (4.04) \end{array} Y_t - \begin{array}{c} 0.7269 \\ (5.91) \end{array} M_t$$

$$+\; \sum_{i=1}^{20} w_i \, pa_i \;,$$

where

$$\sum_{i=1}^{20} w_i \;=\; \begin{array}{c} 0.68 \\ (12.10) \end{array}$$

$$R^2 \;=\; 0.81 \qquad D\text{-}W \;=\; 0.54 \qquad SE \;=\; 1.31$$

Key:
m = yield on one-year Treasury note.
Y = GNP in 1982 dollars.
M = M2 in 1982 dollars.
pa = annualized percent change in the consumer price index.
w = weights with which past rates of inflation
     affect inflation expectations.

Source: Data from the Federal Reserve Board and the U.S. Department
of Commerce. Calculations by the author.

How to Pick a Winner

The timeliness of an indicator is important. Financial markets are captivated for several days each month by announcements of the change in payroll employment and the level of the Purchasing Managers' Index. The two indicators contain some of the earliest available information on the pace of economic activity in the prior month. In contrast, the quarterly report on the U.S. current account balance, which is released with a long lag, attracts little attention.

Second, a tendency toward frequent and large revisions can erode the value of even a very timely indicator. The composite leading economic index is a widely watched gauge of future economic conditions, yet recent research suggests that the often-substantial revisions detract from the value of the index in real-time forecasting exercises.[30]

Of course, the fact that an indicator is subject to revision implies only that more complete information will become available at a later time. A series that is prone to revisions is less timely than the date of its initial release suggests, since final figures are available only with a delay. Even so, the tendency of a series to undergo revisions does not preclude its use as a leading indicator. Many forms of financial market data are in a sense revised continuously, yet are among the most useful indicators of inflation.[31]

Third, difficulty in interpreting a series that is available on a timely basis and is never revised can reduce the value of the series as a leading indicator. For example, in order to extract a signal from a volatile indicator, it may be necessary to transform the data with a statistical smoothing technique.[32] Such methods invariably shorten the lead time of the indicator

Fourth, as discussed in Chapter IV, missed signals and false signals can critically undermine the value of an indicator. In addition, even a time series with a perfect record at turning points is worthless if the lead time is too long and variable. A common criticism of the composite leading economic index, for example, is that its lead time at business cycle peaks has been as short as two months and as long as twenty months.

Finally, a grounding of the relationship between the indicator series and the target series in economic theory provides a basis for assuming, though does not guarantee, that past predictive performance will continue into the future.

The Leading Inflation Index

Coupled with the high and volatile rates of inflation in the last two decades, the notion that inflation expectations play the dominant role in determining nominal interest rates may be responsible for the

outpouring of leading inflation indicators in recent years. The Bank
Credit Analyst publishes a leading inflation index each month in *The
Interest Rate Forecast* and the research departments of many national
securities firms, such as Paine Webber and C. J. Lawrence, have
developed their own indexes.

Roth tested five leading indicators of inflation. The leading
inflation index (LII), produced by the Center for International Business
Cycle Research (CIBCR) at Columbia University, was superior.[33] The
LII is a composite of seven separate economic time series: (1) the
percentage of the working age population employed, (2) debt growth,
(3) the rate of change in industrial materials prices, (4) the rate of
change in import prices (excluding fuels), (5) the expected change in
selling prices from the Dun and Bradstreet survey, (6) the change in
reported buying prices from the National Association of Purchasing
Managers (NAPM) survey, and (7) the supplier deliveries component
of the NAPM survey.[34]

The first three and last two components reflect demand
pressures in the labor, commodities, and capital markets. The percentage of the working age population that is employed measures pressure
on wages, which are widely believed to play a role in inflation. The
rate of increase in industrial materials prices and the two series from
the NAPM survey gauge the influence of economic conditions on
prices.

The Dun and Bradstreet and growth in total debt components are
forward-looking in the sense that they reflect expectations of inflation
pressures and future spending plans, respectively. Import prices are
included to reflect the greater impact of foreign trade on the U.S.
economy.

Over the sample period studied by Roth, the lead time of the
LII was the shortest on average, at 7.7 months, but was the second
most variable, with a standard deviation of 7.4 months. More important
than the direct correspondence between turning points in the indicators
and in inflation, however, is the comparison of the timing of signals
produced from the indicators with the inflation turning points.

On this count, the LII outperformed the other four indicators.
The average lead time was the shortest, at 2.8 months, and the standard
deviation was the lowest among all five indicators.[35] Results from the
examination of the LII over a slightly longer period support these
findings.[36]

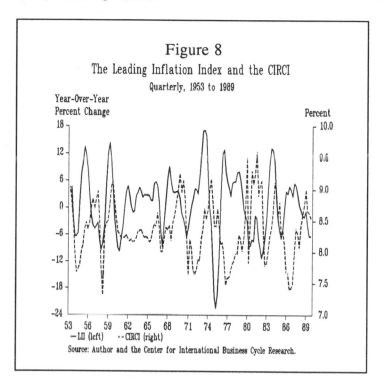

Figure 8
The Leading Inflation Index and the CIRCI
Quarterly, 1953 to 1989

Source: Author and the Center for International Business Cycle Research.

Figure 8 shows a comparison of the year-to-year percent change in the leading inflation index with the CIRCI. Visual examination of the data confirms that the LII consistently changes course in advance of major swings in interest rates, providing further reason to believe that the LII may prove useful in the detection of turning points in the interest rate cycle.

NOTES

1. William Mc C. Martin, before the Ways and Means Committee of the House of Representatives, September 14, 1967, quoted in William E. Gibson, "Price-Expectations Effects on Interest Rates," *Journal of Finance* 25 (March 1970): 19.

2. Henry McMillan and Jerome B. Baesel, "The Role of Demographic Factors in Interest Rate Forecasting," *Managerial and Decision Economics* 9 (September 1988): 187.

3. Knut Wicksell, *Interest and Prices* (London: Macmillan, 1936), 106.

4. Paul A. Samuelson, *Economics* (New York: McGraw-Hill Book Company, 1976), 221, 260-261.

5. John M. Keynes, *A Treatise on Money* 2 (London: Macmillan, 1930), 198-208. Gibson was a British economist who drew attention to the apparent paradox through his studies of the strong and positive correlation between interest rates and prices in England during the 1800s and early 1900s.

6. Irving Fisher, The Theory of Interest (New York: Macmillan, 1930), 399-451.

7. Kajal Lahiri, "Inflationary Expectations: Their Formation and Interest Rate Effects," *American Economic Review* 66 (March 1976), 123.

8. Wicksell, *Interest and Prices*, 103.

9. G. J. Santoni and Courtenay C. Stone, "What Really Happened to Interest Rates?: A Longer-Run Analysis," Federal Reserve Bank of St. Louis *Review* 63 (November 1981): 4.

10. The Hammurabi Code, no. 90, circa 2080 B.C. Quoted in John H. Wood, "Interest Rates and Inflation," Federal Reserve Bank of Chicago *Economic Perspectives* 5 (May/June 1981): 3.

11. Quoted in ibid., 5.

12. Quoted in ibid., 5.

13. Minority Views, Monetary Policy for 1981, Fifth Report by the Committee on Banking, Finance, and Urban Affairs, 97 Congress 1st Session, House Report 97-10, p. 15, quoted in G. J. Santoni and Courtenay C. Stone, "Navigating Through the Interest Rate Morass: Some Basic Principles," Federal Reserve Bank of St. Louis *Review* 63 (March 1981): 18.

14. Studies such as Michael J. Hamburger and William L. Silber, "An Empirical Study of Interest Rate Determination," *Review of Economics and Statistics* 51 (August 1969): 369, which rejects the existence of a link between inflation expectations and nominal interest rates on empirical grounds, and Steven K. McNees, "How Well Do Financial Markets Predict Inflation?" Federal Reserve Bank of Boston *New England Economic Review*, (September/October 1989): 31, which hypothesizes that the myriad of factors affecting real interest rates overshadow the impact of changes in inflation expectations, represent a small minority.

15. Phillip Cagan, "The Monetary Dynamics of Hyper-inflation," in Milton Friedman. ed., *Studies in the Quantity Theory of Money* (Chicago: University of Chicago Press, 1956), 23. Reuben A. Kessel and Armen A. Alchian, "Effects of Inflation," *Journal of Political Economy* 70 (December 1962): 521. Milton Friedman, "Factors Affecting the Level of Interest Rates," in *Current Issues in Monetary Theory and Policy*, 2d ed., ed. Thomas M. Havrilesky and John T. Boorman, (Arlington Heights, Illinois: AHM Publishing Corporation, 1980), 378.

16. Gibson, "Price-Expectations Effects," 33.

17. William E. Gibson, "Interest Rates and Inflationary Expectations: New Evidence," *American Economic Review* 62 (December 1972): 857.

18. Michael Keran and Stephen Zeldes, "Effects of Monetary Disturbances on Exchange Rates, Inflation and Interest Rates," Federal Reserve Bank of San Francisco *Economic Review*, (spring 1980): 7.

19. Charles Pigott, "Indicators of Long-Term Real Interest Rates," Federal Reserve Bank of San Francisco *Economic Review*, (winter 1984): 47.

20. Eugene Fama, "Short-Term Interest Rates as Predictors of Inflation," *American Economic Review* 65 (June 1975): 269.

21. Carl E. Walsh, "Three Questions Concerning Nominal and Real Interest Rates," Federal Reserve Bank of San Francisco *Economic Review*, (fall 1987): 10.

22. David Ranson, "If Real Rates Haven't Changed," *Wall Street Journal*, 3 April 1984, 32.

23. David H. Pyle, "Observed Price Expectations and Interest Rates," *Review of Economics and Statistics* 54 (August 1972): 277.

24. Lahiri, "Inflationary Expectations," 127.

25. Martin Feldstein and Otto Eckstein, "The Fundamental Determinants of the Interest Rate," *Review of Economics and Statistics* 52 (November 1970): 373.

26. William P. Yohe and Denis S. Karnosky, "Interest Rates and Price Level Changes, 1952-69," Federal Reserve Bank of St. Louis *Review* 83 (December 1969): 23. The presence of multicollinearity in unconstrained distributed lag functions can result in large fluctuations in the coefficients, w_i. Use of the Almon lag procedure results in a smoother distribution, which is more consistent with the assumption that inflation expectations are formed adaptively, that is, as a continuous function of past price movements. For details, see Shirley Almon, "The Distributed Lag Between Capital Appropriations and Expenditures," *Econometrica* 33 (January 1965): 178. Equation 13 was estimated using a third-degree polynomial with a length of twenty quarters. Other degree and length selections produced similar results.

27. For the derivation of the functional form, see Thomas J. Sargent, "Commodity Price Expectations and the Interest Rate," *Quarterly Journal of Economics* 83 (February 1969): 130-132.

28. Ibid., 140.

29. Yohe and Karnosky, "Interest Rates," 33. A "beta" coefficient is a coefficient from a linear regression that has been adjusted for the magnitudes of the corresponding explanatory variable and the dependent variable. For further explanation, see Jan Kmenta, *Elements of Econometrics*, 2d ed. (New York: Macmillan, 1986), 422.

30. Francis X. Diebold an Glenn D. Rudebusch, "Ex Ante Turning Point Forecasting with the Composite Leading Index," Finance and Economics Discussion Series no. 40, Federal Reserve Board, Washington, D.C., October 1988.

31. McNees, "How Well Do Financial Markets Predict?" 32

32. Ibid., 33-34.

33. Howard L. Roth, "Leading Indicators of Inflation," Federal Reserve Bank of Kansas City *Economic Review* 71 (November 1986): 3.

34. For a thorough description of the LII, see Geoffrey H. Moore, "An Improved Leading Index of Inflation," manuscript, Center for International Business Cycle Research, Graduate School of Business, Columbia University, New York, October 1988.

35. The means are provided by Roth, "Leading Indicators," 13, 16. The standard deviations were computed from the raw data listed in the tables.

36. John P. Cullity, "Signals of Cyclical Movements in Inflation and Interest Rates," *Financial Analyst's Journal* 43 (September/October 1987): 40.

VI
Sequential Filter Turning Point Forecasts

In forecasting cyclical turning points, a leading index is only as good as the rule used to interpret its movements and map them into turning point predictions.[1]

Much of the difficulty in predicting interest rates arises from an inappropriate approach to the problem. Conventional forecasting methods are ill-suited to anticipating turning points. That is a serious indictment, considering that the crucial test of a forecast lies at the turning point.[2]

The people who make forecasts and those who use them often get a false sense of confidence because forecast errors are not distributed evenly over the business cycle. When the economy is doing well, forecasts that prosperity will continue are usually correct. When the economy is performing poorly, forecasts that the slump will continue are also usually correct. The problem lies in predicting the turning points . . . .[3]

The clear message is that the road to better forecasts is built on the early and reliable recognition of turning points.

IN SEARCH OF A SIGNAL

The process of addressing turning points is a necessary, but not sufficient step toward producing more accurate forecasts. The Commerce Department's system of composite business cycle indicators was designed with specific attention to turning points and has been in widespread use for several decades. Nevertheless, forecasters are humbled by their failures at anticipating recessions. One reason is that an indicator is only as good as the method used for interpretation.[4] Consider the case illustrated in Figure 9.

Panel A shows the monthly patterns of the leading and coincident economic indexes during 1981. Panels B, C, and D show how those patterns looked at various intervals during the year. With the benefit of hindsight, we know that the leading index reached a peak in May. (Panel B) When the May observation became available in June, however, there was no basis for reaching that conclusion.

Even three months later, in September (Panel C), analysts did not yet recognize that the coincident index had reached a cyclical peak in July and that a recession had started in August. By November (Panel D), a downtrend in the coincident index was visible and the decline in the leading index had become pronounced, yet the National Bureau of Economic Research did not designate July 1981 as a reference cycle peak until early 1982.

Despite the fact that the leading index reliably leads the coincident index, the inefficiency of casual observation can overwhelm the information contained in the index. The result is that the message of the leading index can remain ambiguous for many months after a turning point. Under such circumstances, a substantial and costly delay results when the lead time is short, as was the case at the July 1981 business cycle peak.

In an effort to overcome the turning point recognition problem, analysts have proposed a variety of rules for interpreting the leading index. The most well-known is that three consecutive declines spell an imminent economic downturn. The three-drops-and-a-stumble rule serves as a handy shorthand method for recognizing recessions, but suffers several shortcomings.

The rule has no theoretical grounding and is not transferable to other time series or even to identifying business cycle upturns. Moreover, the rule has announced several recessions that did not develop and was late in signaling at least the onset of the 1981 recession.[5]

More sophisticated methods of interpretation have also proved lacking. Hymans used spectral analysis in an only partially successful attempt to ". . . highlight the major cyclical swings [in the leading index] while minimizing the likelihood of false signals."[6] Zarnowitz and Moore developed a system of sequential signals to identify turning

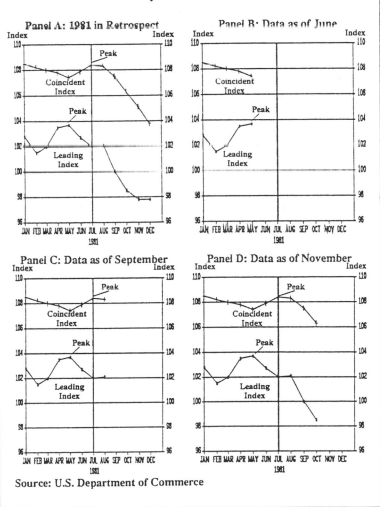

Figure 9
The Case of the Missing Signal
January to December 1981

Source: U.S. Department of Commerce

points ". . . as promptly and accurately as practicable."[7] The Zarno-witz-Moore algorithm for generating a series of turning point signals eliminated the problem of false warnings, but did little to improve the timing of accurate signals.

On a real-time basis in 1981, the Zarnowitz-Moore method did not generate the first of the three signals required to warn of recession until September.[8] The currently available data set, which has undergone several revisions since then, suggests that the third signal did not appear until November 1981.[9]

Progress toward the timely and reliable recognition of business cycle turning points has been slow, despite years of research by scores of prominent scholars. The comparatively unstudied problem of interest rate cycle turning point detection might prove at least as intractable, if not for a branch of statistics called sequential analysis.[10]

SEQUENTIAL ANALYSIS TO THE RESCUE

The process of forecasting turning points in the interest rate cycle is an example of sequential decision making. An analyst obtains and examines observations on the state of interest rates at various intervals. After each observation, the analyst can decide to terminate the sampling process and announce that a turning point has occurred or is about to occur. Alternatively, he can postpone a decision and continue the sampling process.

For example, in light of the inflation-interest rate link, an analyst might decide to forecast a trough in the interest rate cycle after viewing a large increase or a string of small increases in the leading inflation index (LII). Without a formal procedure for mapping indicator values into turning point signals, however, *ad hoc* rules produce unreliable predictions.[11] Witness the three-declines-equals-a-recession rule.

The efficient extraction of information from an indicator is key to the successful detection of turning points. By combining time series methodology with the theory of optimal stopping times, Neftci derived a method for statistically maximizing the use of information in an indicator.[12]

Applying Neftci's Algorithm

One deficiency of other signaling methods is the failure to explicitly incorporate the risk-reward trade-off. Hymans sought to "minimize" false signals, Zarnowitz and Moore to improve the timing of signals as much as "practicable." In the context of both studies, the phrases "minimize" and "as much as 'practicable'" have no special meaning. Loosely translated, the words indicate no more than the intention to do a better job.

Neftci's main contribution was to recognize turning point forecasting as an optimal stopping time problem. It is a stopping time problem because the object of prediction is the time of an event, not the level or rate of change of a time series. The solution is optimal in the sense that the sequential filter allows the analyst to explicitly balance the reward of correctly anticipating a turning point with the risks of sounding a false alarm or issuing a late signal.[13] A chief advantage of the sequential filter is that it optimizes the selection of turning point signals in a statistical sense.

The Framework

Simply stated, the sequential filter is a prediction rule that translates fluctuations of a leading time series into probabilities of a near term turning point in a target time series. A crucial assumption is that the indicator series behaves differently in upturns than in downturns.

The rule requires that the probability distribution that generates the indicator series during upturn regimes is independent of the corresponding distribution for downturn regimes. The sharpness of peaks and troughs in the leading inflation index and the more rapid pace of decreases than of increases are evidence of conformity to the assumption. (See Figure 8 on page 79.)

The sequential filter operates by discerning changes in the stochastic process underlying the indicator series. These switches between probability distributions correspond to regime shifts, and therefore, to turning points. Detection of the otherwise unobservable shifts between the distributions is the mechanism by which the sequential filter produces turning point signals.

The Model

From Shiryayev, the formula to calculate the probability of a near term regime shift, under the above assumptions, is:[14]

$$(14) \qquad P_t = \frac{A}{A + B} ,$$

where

$$A = [P_{t-1} + p^a (1 - P_{t-1})] \, p_t^0 ,$$

$$B = (1 - P_{t-1}) \, p_t^1 \, (1 - p^a) ,$$

P_t is the probability that the stochastic process underlying the leading time series shifted from month *t-1* to month *t*. P_{t-1} is the probability calculated in the prior month. And p^a is the *a priori* probability of a regime switch.

The remaining terms, p_t^0 and p_t^1, are conditional probabilities, based on values of the leading series observed since the last turning point. Their exact natures depend on the prevailing regime. If the most recent turning point was a trough, then p_t^0 and p_t^1 are the conditional probabilities that month *t* was in a downturn regime and an upturn regime, respectively. When the most recent turning point was a peak, p_t^0 and p_t^1 are the conditional probabilities that month *t* was in an upturn regime and a downturn regime, respectively.

The *a priori* probabilities, p^a, or priors, are assigned by the analyst, based on knowledge about the target series, contemporaneous patterns in other indicators, or some other information set. Neftci calculated time-variant priors, based loosely on the average length of post-war business expansions. Others have assumed constant priors, using other criteria. In practice, the P_t are not very responsive to moderate changes in the priors.

APPLICATION TO THE INTEREST RATE CYCLE

The application of the sequential filter involved three steps. First, the conditional density functions for p_t^0 and p_t^1 were estimated. Second, the priors were determined and signal generation criteria were selected. Third, the turning point probabilities, P_t, were calculated recursively for the entire sample period.

Conditional Probability Distributions

The conditional probability distributions, from which p_t^0 and p_t^1 arise, were estimated by classifying the monthly percent changes in the leading inflation index into upturn and downturn regimes. The penalized likelihood method was then used to calculate a nonparametric probability density function for each regime, using the sorted data.[15]

The period April 1953 to December 1988 was divided into upturn and downturn regimes by matching peaks and troughs in the leading inflation index with the corresponding turning points in the CIRCI. For instance, the earliest identified turning point in the CIRCI is a peak in June 1953. The leading inflation index reached a peak the following month, July 1953. The CIRCI reached a trough in July 1954 that was preceded by a trough in the leading inflation index in January 1954. The period from the month following the first identified peak in the leading inflation index (July 1953) to and including the subsequent trough (January 1954) was the first downturn regime. Upturn regimes and the remaining downturn regimes were identified in the same fashion.[16]

Figure 10 shows the observed and smoothed upturn and downturn probability distributions for nodes of 0.1 percentage points. Several observations are in order. The practice of calculating non-parametric distributions differs from published applications of the sequential filter. Neftci used a centered three-term moving average of the observed frequency distributions to provide smoother estimates.[17] Others have fitted normal density functions using sample data.[18]

Smoothness is a desirable property for the conditional probability distributions. For a small sample, the conditional probabilities calculated from observed, unsmoothed distributions will be zero for some nodes. Should p_t^1 equal zero, for example, at the node for a relatively large percentage increase in the leading inflation index during an upturn regime, equation (14) reduces to:

$$(15) \qquad P_t = \frac{A}{A + 0} = 1 .$$

The disturbing result is that for a large increase in the leading inflation index, which would most likely be associated with a trough in interest rates, the probability of a peak is driven to 100 percent.

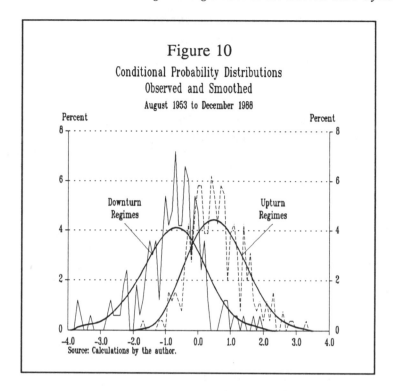

Figure 10

Conditional Probability Distributions
Observed and Smoothed

August 1953 to December 1988

Smooth nonparametric estimates were used instead of fitted functional values because the data do not clearly conform to the normality assumption. Moreover, Neftci argued that ". . . accurate estimation of [the conditional probabilities] is crucial for the success of the method."[19]

Since the Central Limit Theorem[20] offers some support for the normality assumption, the observed frequency distributions for each regime were examined with the chi-squared test and the Lilliefors test for normality.[21] At the 10 percent level of confidence, the Lilliefors test rejected the assumption of normality for the upturn regime and the chi-squared test rejected the assumption of normality for both regimes.

Pick Your Poison

The next step involved determination of the priors. Diebold and Rudebusch argued that, since business expansions are not duration dependent, the priors need not rise as regimes age.[22] They selected the constant prior for each regime that produced the minimum quadratic probability score calculated from a grid search.[23] Shyy assumed that, since the foreign exchange market could be characterized as "bullish" half of the time and "bearish" the other half, 0.5 was a neutral choice for each of the priors.[24]

With respect to the CIRCI, twenty-two turning points occurred during the 429-month period from July 1953 through March 1989, making the observed frequency of turning points of either type approximately 5 percent.[25] Analysts are assumed to have sufficient information to set the priors above 5 percent when appropriate. At the same time, in light of the low frequency of turning points during the sample period, information sources other than the leading inflation index are assumed to regularly imply priors below 50 percent. As a result, constant priors of 27.5 percent—the average of 5 percent and 50 percent—are used.

The next step was specification of the rule used to extract turning point signals from the estimated probabilities. Neftci shows that the optimal stopping time depends on the analyst's willingness to risk a false alarm.[26] Specifically, an imminent turning point is detected when:

$$(16) \qquad P_t \geq 1 - f, \qquad 0 \leq f \leq 1,$$

where f is the acceptable probability of a false signal. In view of the large cost to a bank of making an incorrect interest rate decision, the false signal risk factor is set to 5 percent. In repeated sampling, only five out of every one hundred signals will be false alarms.

The implicit trade-off between timeliness and accuracy is an inescapable feature of forecasting. The certainty associated with a forecast can only be increased at the expense of less timely predictions. With respect to the CIRCI, turning point signals can be issued with complete certainty when the discount rate changes direction. On average, complete certainty at troughs would have come at a cost of 8.5 months and 42.2 percent of the basis point change in yields (100 percent, minus the percentage signaled).

Since $f=.05$, the sequential filter of the leading inflation index will issue a turning point signal when P_t is equal to or greater than 95 percent. Signals that are followed by a reduction in P_t below 95 percent before the occurrence of a turning point will be considered false signals.

In addition, P_{t-1} is set equal to zero in the first month of each regime, since turning points by definition cannot occur in consecutive months. Lastly, following Diebold and Rudebusch, P_{t-1} greater than 95 percent are entered into equation (14) as 95 percent to prevent P_t from rising to 100 percent.[27] If P_t reaches 100 percent, the signal cannot be reversed. For P_{t-1} equal to 100 percent, equation (14) becomes:

$$(17) \qquad P_t = \frac{1}{1+0} = 1 .$$

EMPIRICAL RESULTS

The probability of an imminent turning point in each month of the April 1954 to February 1990 period is illustrated in Figure 11. The vertical lines designate the months of peaks (P) and troughs (T) in the CIRCI. The horizontal lines across the tops of the graphs designate the 95 percent level. The probabilities are graphed for six months after each turning point to allow late signals to register.

In general, the probabilities began each regime at very low levels and rose sharply, exceeding the critical value of 95 percent shortly in advance of most turning points. It is also clear, however, that the sequential filter issued false alarms on occasion. The fourth column in Tables 10a and 10b contains the number and duration of instances in which the probability of an imminent turning point climbed above and then fell below 95 percent in advance of the actual turning point. Two false trough signals were issued for a total of thirteen months. Nine extraneous peak signals were issued for a total of eighteen months.

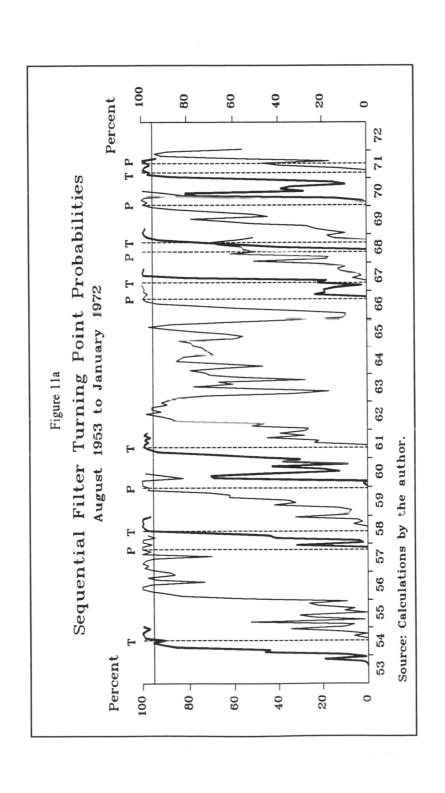

Figure 11a

Sequential Filter Turning Point Probabilities
August 1953 to January 1972

Source: Calculations by the author.

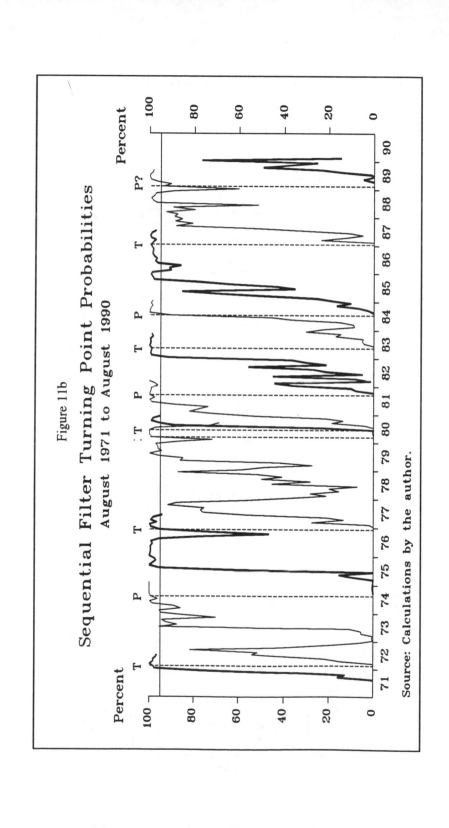

Figure 11b

Sequential Filter Turning Point Probabilities
August 1971 to August 1990

Source: Calculations by the author.

Table 10a
ACCURACY OF SEQUENTIAL FILTER TROUGH
TURNING POINT FORECASTS
JULY 1954 TO JANUARY 1987

Dates of Half Cycles Trough to Peak	Date of Trough Signal	Lead (-)/ Lag (+) in months	False Signals: number/ duration in months	Length of Half Cycle After Signal		Change in CIRCI After Signal	
				in months	% of half cycle	in basis points	% of total change
7/54 - 10/57	8/54	+1	1/1	38	97.4	126	94.0
6/58 - 12/59	6/58	0		18	100.0	180	100.0
5/61 - 9/66	4/61	-1		64	100.0	45	90.0
4/67 - 5/68	7/67	+3		10	76.9	34	58.6
9/68 - 1/70	11/68	+2		14	87.5	100	90.9
3/71 - 7/71	2/71	-1		4	100.0	50	74.6
2/72 - 8/74	1/72	-1		30	100.0	167	99.4
12/76 - 3/80	12/76	0	1/12	39	100.0	125	61.3
6/80 - 9/81	9/80	+3		12	80.0	102	57.6
5/83 - 7/84	2/83	-3		14	100.0	128	97.0
Average		+0.3	2/13	24.3	96.4	106	82.6*

a Average basis point change after signal as a percent of average basis point change over entire half cycle.

Source: Data from the Federal Reserve Board and calculations by the author.

Table 10b
ACCURACY OF SEQUENTIAL FILTER PEAK
TURNING POINT FORECASTS
JULY 1954 TO JANUARY 1987

Dates of Half Cycles Peak to Trough	Date of Peak Signal	Lead (-)/ Lag (+) in months	False Signals: number/ duration in months	Length of Half Cycle After Signal		Change in CIRCI After Signal	
				in months	% of half cycle	in basis points	% of total change
10/57 - 6/58	8/57	-2	3/10	8	100.0	-140	84.8
12/59 - 5/61	11/59	-1		17	100.0	-88	88.9
9/66 - 4/67	8/66	-1	3/3	7	100.0	-74	101.4
5/68 - 9/68	n.s.			0	0.0	0	0.0
1/70 - 3/71	12/69	-1		14	100.0	-159	97.0
7/71 - 2/72	n.s.			0	0.0	0	0.0
8/74 - 12/76	5/74	-3	1/1	28	100.0	-130	74.3
3/80 - 6/80	3/80	0	2/4	3	100.0	-142	84.0
9/81 - 5/83	6/81	-3		20	100.0	-144	80.0
7/84 - 1/87	8/84	+1		29	96.7	-163	94.2
Average		-1.3	9/18	12.6	91.3	-104	79.7[a]

n.s. No signal.
a Average basis point change after signal as a percent of average basis point change over entire half cycle.
Source: Data from the Federal Reserve Board and calculations by the author.

Comparison with Benchmark Forecasts

Even so, the sequential filter performed better than the prime rate rule in this regard. The prime rate rule issued one more false trough alarm than the sequential filter, albeit for seven fewer months. (See Tables 6a and 6b on pages 59 and 60.) With respect to peaks, the prime rate rule generated one less false signal, but for a total of thirty-eight months.

Asleep at the switch? Perhaps more importantly, the sequential filter failed to signal two peaks—May 1968 and July 1971—compared with no missed signals for the prime rate rule. Both turning points, however, occurred after much-shorter-than-average regimes. The first lasted thirteen months and second lasted only four months. The average for the entire sample period was 25.2 months. (See Table 2 on page 43.)

Moreover, the basis point increase in the CIRCI in each case was approximately half or less than the regime average. Indeed, the symmetrical percent changes were the second and third smallest of upturn regimes and the third and fourth smallest of all regimes. In addition, the prime rate signals occurred with only 36 basis points remaining, out of a total move of 107 basis points in the two half cycles. The sequential filter failed, but the costs were small and the prime rate rule did little better.

One possible explanation is that the decreases in interest rates following the two peaks could have resulted from decreases in the real rate of interest, in which case the leading inflation index would have given no warning. Another possibility is that the small size and short duration of the regimes prevented reductions in inflationary pressures from fully registering in the leading inflation index.

The first explanation is more likely. The Survey Research Center at the University of Michigan has measured consumer inflation expectations since 1956.[28] The data are available only quarterly for the period of interest, but suggest that expected inflation actually increased during both regimes. As a consequence, both episodes of decreasing nominal interest rates appear to have resulted from downward adjustments in real rates of interest—developments that the LII would not have detected.

Twice as nice. Judged by the remaining and more important criteria over the entire sample period, the sequential filter of the leading inflation index was vastly superior to both the discount rate and prime rate rules. Discount rate signals lagged 8.5 months behind troughs and 4.2 months behind peaks, occurring with only 66.3 percent and 69.6 percent of the respective regimes remaining. (See Table 5a and 5b on pages 57 and 58.) The prime rate signals were slightly better, lagging 7.8 months and 2.9 months behind trough and peak signals, respectively, and occurring with 67.5 percent and 78.3 percent of the respective regimes remaining. (See Tables 6a and 6b on pages 59 and 60.)

In comparison, the sequential filter signaled troughs in the month of occurrence, on average, lagging by 0.3 months. At peaks, the sequential filter led by 1.3 months. As a result, sequential filter signals announced turning points with 96.4 percent and 91.3 percent of upturn and downturn regimes remaining, respectively. Furthermore, the variation of the sequential filter lead/lag time was much smaller than for either of the naive rules, regardless of whether the long discount and prime rate lags at the May 1961 trough are included.

The most crucial test is the size of the interest rate move that was announced by the signals. On this count, the sequential filter was also far superior to the naive rules. The discount rate rule signaled peaks and troughs with slightly more than half of the move in rates remaining. The prime rate rule was marginally better, signaling peaks with 63.1 percent of the basis point move remaining and troughs with just 57.1 percent left. In contrast, the sequential filter issued trough signals with an average of 82.6 percent of increases in the CIRCI remaining and 79.7 percent of decreases remaining.

On balance, the sequential filter of the leading inflation index issued signals of turning points in the interest rate cycle sooner, more consistently, and with greater profit potential than did the two naive benchmark forecasting rules.

State of rates recognition. The sequential filter also outperformed the market-based predictions of Treasury forward rates and futures rates. Table 11 adds the record of the sequential filter to Table 7. The tables show the percentage of months during which selected forecasting rules correctly indicated the state of interest rates.

The sequential filter correctly identified the prevailing regime slightly more than 80 percent of the time during both the entire sample and the January 1959 to December 1988 sub-sample. In comparison, the discount rate rule scored 72.6 percent and 71.1 percent and the prime rate rule scored 68.0 percent and 66.7 percent, respectively.

The forward rate rule was only half as accurate as the sequential filter, correctly identifying the state of interest rates in fewer than half of the months. In the March 1977 to December 1988 sub-sample, the sequential filter outperformed the forward rate and futures rate rules by a wide margin, but fell to parity with the discount rate and prime rate rules.

Table 11

ACCURACY OF NAIVE AND SEQUENTIAL FILTER
STATE-OF-INTEREST-RATES FORECASTS
SEPTEMBER 1954 TO DECEMBER 1988

Naive Filter	Sample Period		
	9/54 - 12/88	1/59 - 12/88	3/77 - 12/88
Discount Rate	72.6	71.1	79.6
Prime Rate	68.0	66.7	81.7
Forward Rate	n.a.	40.6	48.6
Futures Rate	n.a.	n.a.	54.2
Sequential Filter	80.1	80.3	78.2

n.a. Not available.

Source: Data from the Federal Reserve Board and the *Wall Street Journal* and calculations by the author.

The Current State of Rates

Finally, a note about the tentative interest rate peak in March 1989. The probability of an imminent turning point exceeded 95 percent in July 1988. The reading fell below the critical threshold in November, however, categorizing the period as a four-month false alarm. The probability topped 95 percent again in April 1989, one month after the actual peak. The discount rate has yet to reverse direction, despite the 44 basis point decrease in the CIRCI from March to December 1989.

The prime rate rule produced a signal in June, three months and 33 basis points after the March turning point.

Assuming that March will be confirmed as a peak, the probability of an imminent regime change was near zero from April through July 1989. The odds climbed quickly to approximately 50 percent by October, but receded to 25 percent by year end. In January, the probability increased sharply to 76.7 percent, was still well below the critical level. In February the probability receded to 14.5 percent.

The high January probability may have overstated the chances of a shift to rising rates. The temporary January increase in the LII resulted solely from upward spikes in the two components from the National Association of Purchasing Managers (NAPM) survey. Both measures decreased to near their December levels in February. The unusual pattern in the LII and corresponding spike in the probability apparently resulted from the near-record-cold December weather,[29] which is not a cyclical influence. Moreover, the low February probability indicates that the chances of an imminent cyclical increase in interest rates are low.

Keeping in Touch

Recent experience highlights the value of the interim turning point probabilities produced by the sequential filter. Traditional forecasting techniques provide point predictions, but convey little or no information about the certainty of the estimates. Other methods produce turning point signals, but provide no insight into the chances of witnessing a change of course during the often-long stretches between signals.

In contrast, the sequential filter updates the estimated likelihood of a turning point continuously, as new data become available. To facilitate comparison with benchmark methods, the output from the sequential filter was reduced to dichotomous turning point signals. Since the process underutilizes the information contained in the probabilities, the findings establish a minimum level of performance.

NOTES

1. Diebold and Rudebusch, "Ex Ante Turning Point Forecasting," 2.

2. W. Lee Hoskins, "Breaking the Inflation-Recession Cycle," Federal Reserve Bank of Cleveland *Economic Commentary*, (15 October 1989): 2.

3. Moore, *Business Cycles*, 412.

4. Diebold and Rudebusch, "Ex Ante Turning Point Forecasting," 2.

5. See Gerald H. Anderson and John J. Erceg, "Forecasting Turning Points with Leading Indicators," Federal Reserve Bank of Cleveland *Economic Commentary*, (1 October 1989): 1 for a review of the three declines-equals-a-recession rule.

6. Saul H. Hymans, "On the Use of Leading Indicators to Predict Cyclical Turning Points," *Brookings Papers on Economic Activity*, (2d Quarter 1973): 374.

7. Victor Zarnowitz and Geoffrey H. Moore, "Sequential Signals of Recession and Recovery," *Journal of Business* 55 (January 1982): 75.

8. Ibid., 79.

9. This conclusion is based on the application of Zarnowitz and Moore's method by the Economic Research Department of the Huntington National Bank for use in tracking the U.S. economy on an ongoing basis.

10. See footnote 11 for a listing of sources relating to sequential analysis.

11. In fact, economic forecasters appear to rely on sub-optimal methods. In a clever application of Bayes' theorem, Herman O. Stekler, "An Analysis of Turning Point Forecasts," *American Economic Review* 62 (September 1972): 724 showed that forecasters have routinely underutilized information about the timing of business cycle peaks that is contained in common economic indicators.

12. Salih N. Neftci, "Optimal Prediction of Cyclical Downturns," *Journal of Economic Dynamics and Control* 4 (March 1982): 225.

13. See ibid., 226 for a rigorous discussion of optimality.

14. A. N. Shiryayev, *Optimal Stopping Rules* (New York: Springer-Verlag, 1978): 195. Equation (14) illustrates the independence assumption. Unless p0 and p1 are independently distributed, the equality does not hold.

15. All computations were performed on a Toshiba T3200 personal computer, with SYMPHONY 2.0, Microsoft FORTRAN 5.0, and the DESPL subroutine from the IMSL STAT/LIBRARY 1.0 and under MS-DOS 3.20. For an explanation of the DESPL subroutine and the theory behind it, see IMSL, Inc., *User's Manual: IMSL STAT/LIBRARY FORTRAN Subroutines for Statistical Analysis*, version 1.1 (Houston, 1989), 817 and David W. Scott, "Nonparametric Probability Density Estimation by Optimization Theoretic Techniques," technical report no. 476-131-1, Rice University, Houston, Texas, 1976.

16. The remaining downturn regimes were identified as: December 1955 through April 1958, July 1959 through February 1961, April 1966 through April 1967, March 1968 through September 1968, September 1969 through March 1971, May 1971 through February 1972, November 1973 through December 1976, April 1979 through June 1980, November 1980 through May 1983, June 1984 through January 1987, and the last peak in June 1988 through the end of the sample in December 1988. Upturn regimes comprise the remaining intervals of the sample period.

17. Neftci, "Optimal Prediction," 236.

18. Francis X. Diebold and Glenn D. Rudebusch, "Scoring the Leading Indicators," *Journal of Business* 62 (June 1989): 378; Gang Shyy, "Bullish or Bearish: A Bayesian Dichotomous Model to Forecast Turning Points in the Foreign Exchange Market," *Journal of Economics and Business* 41 (January 1989): 52; and Leonard Mills, "Can Stock Prices Reliably Predict Recessions?" Federal Reserve Bank of Philadelphia *Business Review*, (September/October 1988): 14.

19. Neftci, "Optimal Prediction," 230.

20. Howard E. Reinhardt and Don O. Loftsgaarden, *Elementary Probability and Statistical Reasoning* (Lexington, Massachusetts: D.C. Heath and Company, 1977), 246 explains the Central Limit Theorem.

21. Roger C. Pfaffenberger and James H. Patterson, *Statistical Methods for Business and Economics* (Homewood, Illinois: Richard D. Irwin, 1981), 637-647, 679-680 explains the chi-squared test and Lilliefors test for normality.

22. A stochastic process is duration dependent if the probability of the occurrence of a turning point is an increasing function of the length of the regime. See Francis X. Diebold and Glenn D. Rudebusch, "A Nonparametric Investigation of Duration Dependence in the American Business Cycle," working paper no. 90, Federal Reserve Board, Washington, D.C., November 1988.

23. Diebold and Rudebusch, "Scoring the Leading Indicators," 376-377.

24. Shyy, "Bullish or Bearish, 33.

25. Interest rates are considered to have reached a peak in March 1989, even though the discount rate has not confirmed the occurrence of a turning point.

26. Neftci, "Optimal Prediction," 229.

27. Diebold and Rudebusch, "Scoring the Leading Indicators," 377.

28. Data from the Survey Research Center, Institute for Social Research, The University of Michigan.

29. National Association of Purchasing Management, *Report on Business*, 8 (February 1990): 3-4.

VII
Summary and Conclusions

> Economic forecasters have . . . demonstrated an ability to forecast. But there is much room for improvement, . . . and the most dependable techniques must be developed, demonstrated, and adopted.[1]

Asset-liability managers can augment bank income by skillfully adjusting interest rate exposure. Indeed, management of interest rate risk is a fundamental activity of commercial banks. Moreover, leading institutions view an informed outlook on interest rates as a vital input to asset-liability decisions.

Research, however, has documented the inability of analysts to produce reliable interest rate forecasts. Published interest rate projections are routinely as far as 150 basis points wide of the mark over horizons as short as six months. The record of the experts is no better than that of naive models, but no worse than that of market-based projections.

At the heart of the problem lies an unrealistic objective. Forecasters commonly use time series and econometric techniques to obtain estimates of future interest rate levels. The goal is overly ambitious, and the forecasts are usually stated with an unrealistic degree of precision. Moreover, the methods are ill-suited to the proper objective.

Asset-liability managers are constrained from altering the balance sheet in response to every change in the interest rate outlook. Product volumes and mix can be equally as important as changes in interest rates. In addition, regulatory guidelines and internal investment policies limit discretion.

Consequently, asset-liability managers must nimbly select the most promising chances to capitalize on market developments.

Information about the timing and certainty of significant events in the economy and financial markets is an essential ingredient to the process. The factors of both timing and certainty can be addressed with probability statements.

THE MODEL AND THE TEST

The process of forecasting interest rates involves sequential decision making. The analyst continually gathers information on relevant factors. He can decide at any point to stop sampling and issue a prediction, or he can continue sampling. The theory of optimal stopping times leads to a rule for determining the best time to halt the sampling process, where "best time" has a specific statistical meaning.

The sequential filter translates values of an indicator series into probabilities of the occurrence of a predefined event. Economic theory posits that inflation expectations affect interest rates. Empirical analysis suggests that the role of expected inflation is dominant. The leading inflation index (LII) was selected as the indicator series due to its record of changing course in advance of interest rates, as well as inflation.

The true value of a forecast depends on the quality of the decisions to which it leads. The costs of directly measuring the effects of such decisions, however, are prohibitive. Therefore, the sequential filter was evaluated by comparison with four benchmark methods.

SPECIFIC FINDINGS

By most measures, the sequential filter of the LII outperformed the benchmark forecasts by a wide margin. The sequential filter had the shortest and least variable lead times at both peaks and troughs. Turning point signals were issued with an average of more than 90 percent of half cycles remaining. More importantly, the sequential filter signaled turning points, on average, with approximately 80 percent of the basis point change remaining in the ensuing half cycles.

Benchmark turning point signals were produced from naive rules based on changes of direction in the discount rate and the prime rate. The discount rate rule issued turning point signals with approximately two-thirds of the months and less than five-eighths of the basis point change remaining. The prime rate rule signaled 67.5 percent of the time remaining in upturn regimes and 78.3 percent of the time remaining in downturn regimes. In terms of the change in the CIRCI, the prime rate rule performed little better than the discount rate rule.

Financial markets are widely believed to provide the best possible interest rate forecasts on a consistent basis. Nonetheless, the sequential filter markedly outperformed simple forward rate and futures rate rules for determining the state of interest rates. The sequential filter identified the correct interest rate regime approximately 80 percent of the time. The forward rate and futures rate rules scored 48.6 percent and 54.2 percent, respectively.

CONCLUSIONS

The findings are consistent with the hypothesis that the sequential filter can produce valuable signals of major turning points in the interest rate cycle. In particular, the continuous updating of turning point probability estimates represents a significant advantage over other signal detection methods. Further, the results imply that the technique could have made a meaningful contribution to the process of asset-liability management during much of the post-war period.

The analysis also suggests that the Federal Reserve has adjusted the highly visible and politically charged discount rate more slowly when rates have begun to rise than when rates have begun to fall. This conforms with the notion that monetary policy is a function of the political environment, as well as expected economic and financial developments.

On the other hand, commercial banks have timed adjustments in the prime rate symmetrically at peaks and troughs. This contrasts with the widely held belief that banks are quicker to raise than to lower lending rates.

SUGGESTIONS FOR FURTHER RESEARCH

An important issue for additional research is the variation of signal lead times. A fledgling body of research, which combines monte carlo simulation and regression analysis, represents a promising avenue of investigation. The technique is used to estimate the probability that a predefined event will occur for each month over a forecast horizon of predetermined length.[2] By cumulating monthly estimates, the analyst can compute the probability that a turning point will occur on or before a specific future date.

A second area for further research is the method of calculating the CIRCI. The composition of the index could be tailored to particular markets of relevance to the forecaster, for example. Additionally, the tools of modern time series analysis might improve upon the Commerce Department's procedure for computing composite indexes.[3]

Third, future research can contribute by identifying leading indicators of the interest rate cycle that are available in final form at an early date. In particular, an indicator that reflects movements in the real interest rate, as well as inflation expectations, would prove especially valuable.

Finally, this research has tested the ability of the sequential filter to accurately detect peaks and troughs in the interest rate cycle. In light of the findings, the application of the technique to formulating and implementing investment tactics for commercial banks represents fertile ground for future research.[4]

NOTES

1. Moore, *Business Cycles*, 427.

2. John L. Kling and David A. Bessler, "Calibration-based Predictive Distributions: An Application of Prequential Analysis to Interest Rates, Money, Prices, and Output," *Journal of Business* 62 (April 1989): 477. James H. Stock and Mark W. Watson, "New Indexes," 382 Blanchard and Stanley Fischer (Editors), NBER Macroeconomics Annual 1989 (Cambridge, Massachusetts: The MIT Press, 1989), 382. John L. Kling, "Predicting the Turning Points of Business and Economic Time Series," *Journal of Business* 60 (February 1987): 201. William E. Wecker, "Predicting the Turning Points of a Time Series," *Journal of Business* 52 (January 1979): 35.

3. See Stock and Watson, "New Indexes of Coincident and Leading Economic Indicators."

4. Joel C. Gibbons and Luke D. Knecht, "Interest Rates: A Model with Applications to Active Market Timing," (manuscript, Harris Investment Management Company, Chicago, February 1989), 9 shows how regularly updated probabilistic statements about interest rates can be successfully incorporated into an investment strategy.

Afterword

Since the study presented in this book was completed, it has played a role in preparing interest rate forecasts that have been used in managing interest rate risk at The Huntington National Bank in Columbus, Ohio. Most notably, the high probability of an impending downturn in the interest rate cycle in April 1989 supported the strategy of hedging the bank against an impending downward turn in the interest rate cycle. Figure 11b on page 96 shows that the likelihood of a cyclical turning point in interest rates climbed to 94 percent in February, dipped to 90 percent in March, and then rose beyond the 95 percent threshold to 96 percent in April, reaching 100 percent by June.

But as is often the case near turning points, the future was as uncertain as the stakes were high. The stance in favor of declining interest rates was an unpopular one at the time, because rates had been moving upward for the past year. In fact, the Federal Reserve had just raised the discount rate to 7½ percent on February 24, 1989.

Not surprisingly, the conventional wisdom was that the rising interest rate regime was not about to end. As late as May, the *Blue Chip Financial Forecasts* consensus, for example, was for long term rates to remain essentially flat for the remainder of the year. In particular, more than one-half of the forty-nine panel members expected the 10-year Treasury Note yield to rise or stay the same. A slightly smaller plurality—48 percent—expected the prime rate to be higher or at the same level as in May at the end of the year.[1]

The high probability of a downturn in the interest rate cycle calculated from the sequential filter of the LII was a key element in the decision to adopt and stick with a forecast of declining interest rates early in 1989 and at other times between 1989 and late 1993. On at least three other occasions—following the Gulf War in 1991, in the third quarter of 1992, and in early 1993—perceptions that the economy was gaining momentum sparked inflation

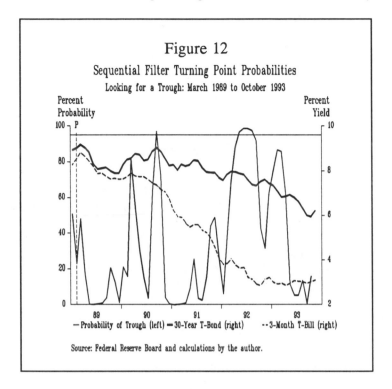

Figure 12

Sequential Filter Turning Point Probabilities

Looking for a Trough: March 1989 to October 1993

Source: Federal Reserve Board and calculations by the author.

fears, which in turn temporarily pushed interest rates higher. The fact that the probability of an upturn in the interest rate cycle remained below the 95 percent threshold with few exceptions, however, was an important factor in maintaining an outlook for still lower yields.

As show in Figure 12, the probability of an upturn in interest rates topped 95 percent in August 1990, reflecting the spike in oil prices related to the Persian Gulf Conflict. At the time, it was discounted as an anomaly because of its cause. A more serious string of four upturn signals occurred from May to August 1992, preceded a 71 basis point rise in the yield on the 30-year Treasury Bond from 7.05 percent on September 4 to 7.76 percent on November 6. Yet this increase gave way to renewed and sharp decline in short order, rendering the four-month signal a false warning of a cyclical upturn in rates.

Nonetheless, the sequential probabilities of impending turning points in the interest rate cycle have provided valuable support in the preparation of interest rate forecasts since this study was completed. In almost all months during the 1989-1993 period, during which long rates decreased by about 300 basis points and short rates declined by approximately 600 basis points, the sequential filter probabilities pointed steadfastly in the direction of lower rates.

NOTES

1. *Blue Chip Financial Forecasts*, (Alexandria, Virginia) 8, no. 1 (January 1, 1989): 2-6.

Bibliography

Ahlers, David and Lakonishok, Josef. "A Study of Economists' Consensus Forecasts," *Management Science*, 29 (October 1983): 1113.

Almon, Shirley. "The Distributed Lag Between Capital Appropriations and Expenditures," *Econometrica*, 33 (January 1965): 178.

Anderson, Gerald H. and Erceg, John J. "Forecasting Turning Points with Leading Indicators," Federal Reserve Bank of Cleveland *Economic Commentary*, (October 1, 1989): 1.

The Bank Credit Analyst, "Preconditions for an Interest Rate Peak," *Investment and Business Forecast*, 40 (March 1989): 5.

Belongia, Michael T. "Predicting Interest Rates," Federal Reserve Bank of St. Louis *Review*, 69 (March 1987): 9.

———— and Santoni, Gary J. "Interest Rate Risk, Market Value, and Hedging Financial Portfolios," *Journal of Financial Research*, 10 (spring 1987): 47.

Blanchard, Oliver Jean and Fischer, Stanley, ed. *NBER Macroeconomics Annual 1989*. Cambridge, Massachusetts: The MIT Press, 1989.

Blue Chip Financial Forecasts. (Alexandria, Virginia) 8, no. 1 (January 1, 1989).

Bolton, A. Hamilton. *Money and Investment Profits*. Homewood, Illinois: Dow Jones-Irwin, 1967.

Boschan, Charlotte and Bry, Gerhard. "Cyclical Analysis of Time Series: Selected Procedures and Computer Programs," technical paper no. 20, National Bureau of Economic Research, 1971.

———— and Ebanks, Walter W. "The Phase-Average Trend: A New Way of Measuring Economic Growth," in Proceedings of the Business and Statistics Section, proceedings of a conference sponsored by the American Statistical Association. Washington, D.C., 1978, 332.

Bowsher, Norman N. "Rise and Fall of Interest Rates," Federal Reserve Bank of St. Louis *Review*, 62 (August/September 1980): 16.

Burger, Albert E., Lang, Richard W. and Rasche, Robert H. "The Treasury Bill Futures Market and Market Expectations of Interest Rates," Federal Reserve Bank of St. Louis *Review*, 59 (June 1977): 2.

Burns, Arthur F. and Mitchell, Wesley C. *Business Cycles: The Problem and Its Setting*. New York: National Bureau of Economic Research, 1927.

————. Measuring Business Cycles. New York: National Bureau of Economic Research, 1946. Cagan, Phillip. "Changes in the Cyclical Behavior of Interest Rates," National Bureau of Economic Research, Occasional Paper 100, 1969.

————. "The Recent Cyclical Movements of Interest Rates in Historical Perspective," *Business Economics*, 7 (January 1972): 43.

Chicago Mercantile Exchange. *Opportunities in Interest Rates: Treasury Bill Futures*. 2d ed. Chicago, 1979. Cullity, John P. "Signals of Cyclical Movements in Inflation and Interest Rates," *Financial Analyst's Journal*, 43 (September/October 1987): 40.

Cyert, Richard M. and DeGroot, Morris H. *Bayesian Analysis and Uncertainty in Economic Theory*. Towtowa, New Jersey: Rowman and Littlefield, 1987.

Diebold, Francis X. and Rudebusch, Glenn D. "A Non- parametric Investigation of Duration Dependence in the American Business Cycle," Economic Activity Working Paper no. 90, Federal Reserve Board, November 1988.

————. "Ex Ante Turning Point Forecasting with the Composite Leading Index," Finance and Economics Discussion Series no. 40, Federal Reserve Board, Washington, D.C., October 1988.

————. "Scoring the Leading Indicators," *Journal of Business*, 62 (June 1989): 369.

Dua, Pami, "Multiperiod Forecasts of Interest Rates," *Journal of Business and Economic Statistics*, 6, (July 1988): 381.

Ellig, Jerome. "For Better Weather, Privatize," *Wall Street Journal*, 4 December 1989, sec. A, p. 14.

Fama, Eugene F. "Short-Term Interest Rates as Predictors of Inflation," *American Economic Review*, 65 (June 1975): 269.

————. "The Information in the Term Structure," *Journal of Financial Economics*, 13 (December 1984b): 509.

Feldstein, Martin and Eckstein, Otto. "The Fundamental Determinants of the Interest Rate," *Review of Economics and Statistics*, 52 (November 1970): 363.

Fels, Rendigs and Hinshaw, C. Elton. *Forecasting and Recognizing Business Cycle Turning Points*. New York: National Bureau of Economic Research, 1968.

Fisher, Irving. "Appreciation and Interest," *Publications of the American Economic Association*, 11 (August 1896): 23.

————. *The Theory of Interest*. New York: Macmillan, 1930.

Fitzgerald, Terry J. and Miller, Preston J. "A Simple Way to Estimate Current-Quarter GNP," *Federal Reserve Bank of Minneapolis Quartery Review*, 13 (fall 1989): 27.

Fraser, Donald R. "On the Accuracy and Usefulness of Interest Rate Forecasts," *Business Economics*, 12 (September 1977): 38.

Friedman, Benjamin M. "Interest Rate Expectations Versus Forward Rates: Evidence From an Expectations Survey," *Journal of Finance*, 34 (September 1979): 965.

————. "Survey Evidence on the 'Rationality' of Interest Rate Expectations," *Journal of Monetary Economics*, 6 (October 1980): 453.

Friedman, Milton, ed. *Studies In the Quantity Theory of Money*. Chicago: University of Chicago Press, 1956.

"Gap Management Eases Interest Rate Swings," *Savings Institutions*, 109 (November 1988): 44.

Gibbons, Joel C. and Knecht, Luke D. "Interest Rates: A Model with Applications to Active Market Timing," Harris Investment Management Company, Chicago, manuscript, February 1989.

Gibson, William E. "Interest Rates and Inflationary Expectations: New Evidence," *American Economic Review*, 62 (December 1972): 854.

————. "Price-Expectations Effects on Interest Rates," *Journal of Finance*, 25 (March 1970): 19.

Giordano, Robert M. "Interest Rate Outlook." *The Pocket Chartroom* (The Goldman Sachs Economic Research Group), no. 4 (April 1989): C5.

Gordon, Robert J., ed. *The American Business Cycle: Continuity and Change.* Chicago and London: University of Chicago Press, 1986.

Grossman, Sanford S. and Stiglitz, Joseph E. "On the Impossibility of Informationally Efficient Markets," *American Economic Review,* 70 (June 1980): 393.

Guttentag, Jack M., ed. *Essays on Interest Rates.* Vol. 2. New York: National Bureau of Economic Research, 1971.

———— and Cagan, Phillip, ed. *Essays on Interest Rates.* Vol. 1. New York: National Bureau of Economic Research, 1969.

Hafer, R. W. and Hein, Scott E. "Comparing Futures and Survey Forecasts of Near-Term Treasury Bill Rates," *Federal Reserve Bank of St. Louis Review,* 71 (May/June 1989): 33.

Hamburger, Michael J. and Silber, William L. "An Empirical Study of Interest Rate Determination," *Review of Economics and Statistics,* 51 (August 1969): 369.

Havrilesky, Thomas M. and Boorman, John T., ed. *Current Issues in Monetary Theory and Policy.* 2d ed. Arlington Heights, Illinois: AHM Publishing Corporation, 1980.

Hedge, S. P. and MacDonald, B. "On the Informational Role of Treasury Bill Futures," *Journal of Futures Markets,* 6 (winter 1986): 629.

Henry, George B. "Wall Street Economists: Are They Worth Their Salt?" *Business Economics,* 24 (October 1989): 44.

Hertzberg, Marie P. and Beckman, Barry A. "Business Cycle Indicators: Revised Composite Indexes," *Business Conditions Digest,* 29 (January 1989): 97.

Hicks, John R. *Value and Capital.* London: Clarendon Press, 1939.

Homer, Sidney. *A History of Interest Rates.* 2d ed. New Brunswick, New Jersey: Rutgers University Press, 1977.

Hoskins, W. Lee. "Breaking the Inflation-Recession Cycle," *Federal Reserve Bank of Cleveland Economic Commentary,* (October 15, 1989): 2.

Howard, C. T. "Are T-Bill Futures Good Forecasters of Interest Rates?" *Journal of Futures Markets,* 1 (winter 1982): 305.

House Committe on Appropriations. *Testimony of Arthur Burns.* 93d Congress, 1st sess., 21 February 1974.

Hymans, Saul H. "On the Use Leading Indicators to Predict Cyclical
   Turning Points," *Brookings Papers on Economic Activity*,
   (2d Quarter 1973): 339.
IMSL, Inc. *User's Manual: IMSL STAT\LIBRARY FORTRAN Sub-*
   routines for Statistical Analysis, version 1.1. Houston, 1989.
Jasen, Georgette and Herman, Tom. "How Managers Predict Direc-
   tion of Rates," *Wall Street Journal* (New York) 7 February
   1989, sec. C, p. 1.
Kamara, A. and Lawrence, C. "The Information Content of the
   Treasury Bill Futures Market Under Changing Monetary
   Regimes," working paper no. 51, University of Michigan,
   1986.
Kane, Edward J. and Malkiel, Burton G. "The Term Structure of
   Interest Rates: An Analysis of a Survey of Interest-Rate
   Expectations," *Review of Economics and Statistics*, 49
   (August 1967): 343.
Keran, Michael and Zeldes, Stephen. "Effects of Monetary Distur-
   bances on Exchange Rates, Inflation and Interest Rates,"
   Federal Reserve Bank of San Francisco *Economic Review*,
   (spring 1980): 7.
Kessel, Reuben A. "The Cyclical Behavior of the Term Structure of
   Interest Rates," occasional paper no. 91, National Bureau of
   Economic Research, December 1965.
—— and Alchian, Armen A. "Effects of Inflation," *Journal of*
   Political Economy, 70 (December 1962): 521.
Keynes, John M. *A Treatise on Money*. Vol. 2. London: Macmillan,
   1930.
Klein, Lawrence R. "The Importance of the Forecast," *Journal of*
   Forecasting, 3 (January/March 1984): 1.
Kling, John L. "Predicting the Turning Points of Business and
   Economic Time Series," *Journal of Business*, 60 (February
   1987): 201.
—— and Bessler, David A. "Calibration-based Predictive Distri-
   butions: An Application of Prequential Analysis to Interest
   Rates, Money, Prices, and Output," *Journal of Business*, 62
   (April 1989): 477.
Kmenta, Jan. *Elements of Econometrics*. 2d ed. New York: Mac-
   millan, 1986.

Kopcke, Richard W. "Inflation, Taxes, and Interest Rates," Federal
    Reserve Bank of Boston New England *Economic Review*,
    (July/August 1988): 3.
Lahiri, Kajal. "Inflationary Expectations: Their Formation and
    Interest Rate Effects," *American Economic Review*, 66
    (March 1976): 124.
Lang, Richard W. and Rasche, Robert H. "A Comparison of Yields
    On Futures Contracts and Implied Forward Rates," Federal
    Reserve Bank of St. Louis *Review*, 60 (December 1978):
    21.
MacDonald, Scott S. and Hein, Scott E. "Futures Rates and Forward
    Rates as Predictors of Near-Term Treasury Bill Rates,"
    Journal of Futures Markets, 9 (June 1989): 250.
Malkiel, Burton G. *The Term Structure of Interest Rates: Expecta-
    tions and Behavior Patterns*. Princeton, New Jersey: Prince-
    ton University Press, 1966.
Mankiw, Gregory N. and Summers, Lawrence H. "Do Long-Term
    Interest Rates Overreact to Short-Term Interest Rates?"
    Brookings Papers on Economic Activity, (First Quarter
    1984): 223.
McMillan, Henry and Baesel, Jerome B. "The Role of Demographic
    Factors in Interest Rate Forecasting," *Managerial and
    Decision Economics*, 9 (September 1988): 187.
McNees, Steven K. "Forecasting Accuracy of Alternative Tech-
    niques: A Comparison of U.S. Macroeconomic Forecasts,"
    Journal of Business and Economic Statistics, 4 (January
    1986): 5.
————. "Forecasting Cyclical Turning Points: The Record in the
    Past Three Recessions," Federal Reserve Bank of Boston
    New England Economic Review, (March/April 1987): 31.
————. "How Accurate Are Macroeconomic Forecasts?" Federal
    Reserve Bank of Boston *New England Economic Review*,
    (July/August 1988): 15.
————. "How Well Do Financial Markets Predict Inflation?" Feder-
    al Reserve Bank of Boston *New England Economic Review*,
    (September/October 1989): 30.
————. "Modeling the Fed: A Forward-Looking Monetary Policy
    Reaction Function," Federal Reserve Bank of Boston *New
    England Economic Review*, (November/December 1986): 3.

Meiselman, David. *The Term Structure of Interest Rates.* Englewood Cliffs, New Jersey: Prentice Hall, 1962.

Melton, William C. *Inside the Fed: Making Monetary Policy.* Homewood, Illinois: Dow Jones-Irwin, 1985.

Mills, Leonard. "Can Stock Prices Reliably Predict Recessions?" Federal Reserve Bank of Philadelphia *Business Review*, (September/October 1988): 3.

Mincer, Jacob, ed. *Economic Forecasts and Expectations: Analyses of Forecasting Behavior and Performance.* New York: National Bureau of Economic Research, 1969.

Mitchell, Wesley C. *Business Cycles and Their Causes.* Berkeley: University of California Press, 1941.

Mintz, Ilse. "Dating United States Growth Cycles," *Explorations in Economic Research*, 1 (summer 1974): 1.

Moore, Geoffrey H. "An Improved Leading Index of Inflation," Center for International Business Cycle Research, Graduate School of Business, Columbia University, manuscript, October 1988.

――――. *Business Cycles, Inflation, and Forecasting.* New York: National Bureau of Economic Research, 1983.

National Association of Purchasing Management. *Report on Business*, 8 (February 1990)

Neftci, Salih N. "Are Economic Time Series Asymmetric over the Business Cycle?" *Journal of Political Economy*, 92 (February 1984): 307.

――――. "Lead-Lag Relations, Exogeneity and Prediction of Economic Time Series," *Econometrica*, 47 (January 1979): 101.

――――. "Optimal Prediction of Cyclical Downturns," *Journal of Economic Dynamics and Control*, 4 (March 1982): 225.

Palash, Carl J. and Radecki, Lawrence J. "Using Monetary and Financial Variables to Predict Cyclical Downturns," Federal Reserve Bank of New York *Quarterly Review*, 10 (summer 1985): 36.

Pankratz, Alan. "Forecasting Financial Market Cycles with Optimal Filtering and Stopping Time Analysis," Department of Economics, DePauw University, manuscript, April 1987.

Pfaffenberger, Roger C. and Patterson, James H. *Statistical Methods for Business and Economics.* Homewood, Illinois: Richard D. Irwin, 1981.

Pigott, Charles. "Indicators of Long-Term Real Interest Rates," Federal Reserve Bank of San Francisco *Economic Review*, (winter 1984): 45.

Poole, William. "Using T-Bill Futures to Gauge Interest-Rate Expectations," Federal Reserve Bank of San Francisco *Economic Review*, (spring 1978): 7.

Prell, Michael J., "How Well Do the Experts Forecast Interest Rates?" Federal Reserve Bank of Kansas City *Monthly Review*, 58 (September/October 1973): 3.

Pring, Martin J. *How to Forecast Interest Rates*. New York: McGraw-Hill Book Company, 1981.

Prochnow, Herbert V., ed. *The Five-Year Outlook for Interest Rates*. Chicago: Rand McNally and Company, 1968.

Pyle, David H. "Observed Price Expectations and Interest Rates," *Review of Economics and Statistics*, 54 (August 1972): 275.

Ramsey, James B. *Economic Forecasting — Models or Markets?*, CATO Paper No. 10. San Francisco: CATO Institute, 1980.

Ranson, David. "If Real Interest Rates Haven't Changed," *Wall Street Journal* (New York) 3 April 1984, 32.

Ratti, Ronald A. "A Descriptive Analysis of Economic Indicators," Federal Reserve Bank of St. Louis *Review*, 67 (January 1985): 14.

Reinhardt, Howard E. and Loftsgaarden, Don O. *Elementary Probability and Statistical Reasoning*. Lexington, Massachusetts: D.C. Heath and Company, 1977.

Roll, Richard. *The Behavior of Interest Rates*. New York: Basic Books, 1970.

Roth, Howard L. "Leading Indicators of Inflation," Federal Reserve Bank of Kansas City *Economic Review*, 71 (November 1986): 3.

Santoni, G. J. and Stone, Courtenay C. "What Really Happened to Interest Rates?: A Longer-Run Analysis," Federal Reserve Bank of St. Louis *Review*, 63 (November 1981): 3.

————. "Navigating Through The Interest Rate Morass: Some Basic Principles," Federal Reserve Bank of St. Louis *Review*, 63 (March 1981): 11.

Sargent, Thomas J. "Commodity Price Expectations and the Interest Rate," *Quarterly Journal of Economics*, 83 (February 1969): 127.

Scott, David W. "Nonparamteric Probability Density Estimation by Optimization Theoretic Techniques," technical report no. 476-131-1, Rice University, Houston, Texas, 1976.

Sebastian, Pamela. "Predictor's Peril: Short One Recession, Wall Street Economist Hits a Bumpy Stretch," *Wall Street Journal* (New York): October 30, 1989, A1.

Shiller, Robert J., Campbell, John Y. and Schoenholtz, Kermit L. "Forward Rates and Future Policy: Interpreting the Term Structure of Interest Rates," *Brookings Papers on Economic Activity*, (First Quarter 1982): 173.

Shiryayev, A. N. *Optimal Stopping Rules*. New York: Springer-Verlag, 1978.

Shiskin, Julius. "Signals of Recession and Recovery: An Experiment with Monthly Reporting," National Bureau of Economic Research, Occasional Paper 77, 1961.

Shyy, Gang. "Bullish or Bearish. A Baycsian Diohotomous Model to Forecast Turning Points in the Foreign Exchange Market," *Journal of Economics and Business*, 41 (January 1989): 49.

Simons, Katerina. "Measuring Credit Risk in Interest Rate Swaps." Federal Reserve Bank of Boston *New England Economic Review*, (November/October 1989): 29.

Stekler, Herman O. "An Analysis of Turning Point Forecasts," *American Economic Review*, 62 (September 1972): 724.

———. "An Evaluation of Quarterly Judgmental Economic Forecasts," *Journal of Business*, 41 (July 1968): 329.

Stigum, Marsha L. and Branch, Rene O., Jr. *Managing Bank Assets and Liabilities*. Homewood, Illinois: Dow Jones-Irwin, 1983.

Stock, James H. and Watson, Mark W. "A Probability Model of the Coincident Economic Indicators," working paper no. 2772, National Bureau of Economic Research, November 1988.

Strongin, Steven and Binkley, Paula S. "A Policymaker's Guide to Economic Forecasts," Federal Reserve Bank of Chicago *Economic Perspectives*, 12 (May/June 1988): 3.

Thornton, Daniel, L. "The Discount Rate and Market Interest Rates: What's the Connection?" Federal Reserve Bank of St. Louis *Review*, 64 (June/July 1982): 3.

Throop, Adrian W. "Interest Rate Forecasts and Market Efficiency,"
    Federal Reserve Bank of San Francisco *Economic Review*,
    (spring 1981): 29.

U.S. Department of Commerce, *The Handbook of Cyclical Indica-
    tors*. Washington, D.C.: U.S. Government Printing Office,
    1984.

Vasciek, Oldrich A. and McQuown, John A. "The Efficient Market
    Method," *Financial Analysts Journal*, 28 (September 1972):
    75.

Walsh, Carl E. "Three Questions Concerning Nominal and Real
    Interest Rates," Federal Reserve Bank of San Francisco
    Economic Review, (fall 1987): 5.

Watson, Mark, Department of Economics, Northwestern University.
    "The New Leading Indicators and Recession Index," a
    presentation to the Fourth Federal Reserve District Econom-
    ic Roundtable, Cleveland, Ohio, 26 January 1990.

Weberman, Ben. "Smart Answers to Dumb Questions," *Forbes*, 19
    May 1986, 110.

Wecker, William. "Predicting the Turning Points of a Time Series,"
    Journal of Business, 52 (January 1979): 35.

Wetherill, G. Barrie and Glazebrook, Kevin D. *Sequential Methods
    in Statistics*. 3d ed. London: Chapman and Hall, 1986.

Wicksell, Knut, *Interest and Prices*. London: Macmillan, 1936.

Wilson, Paul H. "Can Interest Rates Really Be Predicted?" *Pension
    World*, 23 (May 1987): 18.

Wood, John H. "Interest Rates and Inflation," Federal Reserve Bank
    of Chicago *Economic Perspectives*, 5 (May/June 1981): 3.

Worley, Richard B. and Diller, Stanley. "Interpreting the Yield
    Curve," Goldman Sachs Economics, Research Report,
    September 1976.

Yohe, William and Karnosky, Denis S. "Interest Rates and Price
    Level Changes, 1952-1969," Federal Reserve Bank of St.
    Louis *Review*, 83 (December 1969): 18.

Zarnowitz, Victor. "The Accuracy of Individual and Group Fore-
    casts from Business Outlook Surveys," *Journal of Forecast-
    ing*, 3 (January/March 1984): 11.

————, ed. *The Business Cycle Today*. New York: Columbia
    University Press for the National Bureau of Economic
    Research, 1972.

———— and Lambros, Louis A. "Consensus and Uncertainty in Economic Prediction," *Journal of Political Economy*, 95 (June 1987): 591.

————. "Rational Expectations and Macroeconomic Forecasts," working paper no. 1070, National Bureau of Economic Research, January 1983.

————. "The Record and Improvability of Economic Forecasting," reprint no. 880, National Bureau of Economic Research, June 1987.

———— and Moore, Geoffrey H. "Sequential Signals of Recession and Recovery," *Journal of Business*, 55 (January 1982): 57.

Index

About the author

James W. Coons is Vice President and Chief Economist for The Huntington National Bank, headquartered in Columbus, Ohio. His responsibilities include tracking and analyzing the economies of the Midwest and the nation. Mr. Coons monitors and writes on issues related to banking, prepares regular forecasts of economic activity and interest rates, and advises senior management of The Huntington on asset-liability and investment strategy.

Mr. Coons earned a B.A. in economics and mathematics at DePauw University and graduated first in his class with an M.A. in economics from Ohio University. He ranked number one and graduated "With Distinction" from the American Bankers Association's Stonier Graduate School of Banking, where his thesis on predicting interest rates received the prestigious Library Award.

James W. Coons is a founding member and Treasurer of the Columbus Association of Business Economists and serves on the American Bankers Association's Economic Advisory Committee and the Ohio Governor's Economic Advisory Council. He is a contributor to the *Blue Chip Financial Forecasts* interest rate forecasting panel and the Fourth Federal Reserve District Economists Roundtable and is a member of the American Economic Association and the National Association of Business Economists.